Work and Families
2007

Revised and updated by
Lynda A C Macdonald

Croner
a Wolters Kluwer business

Wolters Kluwer (UK) Limited
145 London Road
Kingston upon Thames
Surrey KT2 6SR
Tel: 020 8247 1175

Published by
Wolters Kluwer (UK) Limited
145 London Road
Kingston upon Thames
Surrey KT2 6SR
Tel 020 8247 1175

First published April 2002
Second Edition 2005
Third Edition 2007

Although great care has been taken in the compilation and preparation of this
book to ensure accuracy, the publishers cannot in any circumstances accept
responsibility for any errors or omissions.

Readers of this book should be aware that only Acts of Parliament and
Statutory Instruments have the force of law and that only the courts can
authoritatively interpret the law.

British Library cataloguing in Publication Data. A CIP Catalogue Record for
this book is available from the British Library

ISBN 978–1–85524–701–7

Printed by Legoprint — Lavis(TN), Italy

Contents

1. Why Implement Family-friendly Policies?

Introduction   1

Legal Requirements — a Summary   1

Best Practice   2

The Business Case   7

2. Maternity Policies, Leave and Associated Issues

Introduction   13

Legal Requirements — a Summary   14

Time Off for Antenatal Care   14

Rights to Paid Suspension from Work on Health
  and Safety Grounds   16

Maternity Leave   17

Statutory Maternity Pay   19

Employees' Rights During Maternity Leave   21

Right to Return to Work   23

Temporary Replacements   25

Protection from Detriment and Dismissal   26

Continuity of Service   27

Future Developments   27

Devising a Maternity Policy   28

Sample Policies   35

Key Facts   39

3. Paternity Policies, Leave and Associated Issues

Introduction   43

Legal Requirements — a Summary   43

Paternity Leave   44

Statutory Paternity Pay   46

Future Developments   47

Sample Policy   48

Key Facts   50

4. Adoption Policies, Leave and Associated Issues
Introduction   51
Legal Requirements — a Summary   51
Adoption Leave   52
Statutory Adoption Pay   54
Employees' Rights During Adoption Leave   56
Right to Return to Work   57
Protection from Detriment and Dismissal   59
Sample Policies   59
Key Facts   62
5. Parental Leave
Introduction   65
Legal Requirements — a Summary   65
Parental Leave Entitlements   66
Parental Leave Schemes   69
Contractual Right to Parental Leave   71
Record Keeping   71
Detriment and Dismissal   72
Enforcement   72
Best Practice   72
Key Facts   73
6. Time Off Work to Care for Dependants
Introduction   75
Legal Requirements — a Summary   75
Entitlement to Time Off Work to Care for
    Dependants   75
Detriment and Dismissal   78
Enforcement   78
Sample Policy   78
Key Facts   79
7. Other Types of Leave
Introduction   81

Compassionate Leave 81
Sample Policy 85
Career Breaks 85
Sample Policy 93
Key Facts 95

8. Childcare and Dependant Care
Introduction 97
Provision of Childcare 97
Employer Initiatives and Tax Treatment 99
Best Practice 101
Caring for other Dependants 104
Sample Policy 104
Key Facts 105

9. Flexible Working Patterns
Introduction 107
Part-time Working 108
Sample Policy Statement 112
Job-sharing 112
Compressed Hours 114
Term-time Working 114
Annualised Hours 116
Homework and Telework 119
Flexible Working Hours and Flexitime 123
Sample Policy 126
Key Facts 126

10. Right to Request Flexible Working
Introduction 129
Eligibility to Request Flexible Working 129
Types of Request for Flexible Working 130
Procedure for Considering a Request 131
Reasons for Refusing a Request 132
Enforcement 133

Detriment or Dismissal 133
Sample Policy 134
Key Facts 135

CHAPTER 1

WHY IMPLEMENT FAMILY-FRIENDLY POLICIES?

INTRODUCTION

Employers are increasingly under an obligation to offer their employees more family-friendly working conditions and much has been said and written about the benefits to business of flexible working patterns. Furthermore, recent legislation has added substantially to employees' rights in this area. It makes sound business sense for employers to adopt a positive approach towards family-friendly working practices and look proactively at how flexible working patterns could be implemented within their organisations.

LEGAL REQUIREMENTS — A SUMMARY

Legislation granting rights to employees who are parents has been substantially strengthened in recent years. In addition to longer periods of maternity leave for female employees (see Chapter 2), there are now rights for:

- new fathers to take paternity leave (see Chapter 3)
- adoptive parents to take adoption leave (see Chapter 4)
- parents of a child under five to take unpaid parental leave (see Chapter 5)
- all workers to take reasonable time off work to care for dependants (see Chapter 6), and
- the parents of a child under six and the carers of adult dependants to lodge a request for flexible working (see Chapter 10).

BEST PRACTICE

The term "family-friendly" was widely used during the 1990s to describe flexible working practices. Initially the issue was about working mothers taking care of young children and combining this role with their working lives.

In recent years, however, there has been a shift in focus from the role of the working mother to that of the parents, especially fathers, in family life, and how work impacts on fathers as well as mothers. The emotional as well as the financial responsibilities of fathers towards their families have begun to be recognised. It is increasingly accepted that not only do fathers have an important role in bringing up their children, but also that there is a need to enable them to fulfil it to a greater extent than has in the past been possible. On another front, demographic trends indicate that in the next 10 or so years, the dependant elderly will outnumber the dependant young. By 2010, one fifth of the population could be caring for elderly or disabled relatives. Most employers have yet to introduce support for employees who look after frail, disabled or ill dependants of any age.

The trend is towards an ever-ageing population, a higher proportion of women in full-time employment and a dramatic increase in lone parents and carers, all with responsibilities outside the workplace and a pressing need to balance those with their working lives.

It follows that juggling paid work and caring responsibilities is not only about working women, but it is about men and women caring for dependants, whether young, old or disabled. Family-friendly policies are now maturing into the concept of the "work-life balance". This is about adjusting working patterns so that everyone, regardless of gender, age, race or any other personal factor can find a rhythm that enables them more easily to combine work with their responsibilities for home and family. Taken a step further, the term embraces employees' aspirations outside of work as well as those related to their careers or jobs. It is about allowing employees to have (within reason) some choices as to their working patterns so as to fit in with their personal lives and interests outside of work.

It may sound as though this approach is all about responding to the needs of the workforce. This highlights the underlying question: is it about responding to the needs of the workforce or is it about responding to business needs? The answer is in fact a bit of both.

Research commissioned by Carers UK and conducted by Sheffield Hallam University found that adopting flexible working practices helped organisations achieve several benefits including:

- better ability to attract and retain skilled staff
- a reduction in employee stress and sickness absence
- a significant increase in productivity
- improved service delivery.

The research also found that implementing flexible working practices need not be expensive, particularly when compared to the cost of recruiting and training new staff.

According to the research, three million people combine work and caring responsibilities and carers represent one in eight employees in the UK workforce. The survey, titled "Who Cares Wins", is available at *www.acecarers.org/uk*.

This chapter focuses on family-friendly policies, which for most employers is still the term they are familiar with and use to describe the policies and practices they implement in this area. The remaining chapters cover the following areas:

- maternity policies, leave and associated issues
- paternity policies, leave and associated issues
- adoption policies, leave and associated issues
- parental leave
- time off work to care for dependants
- other types of family leave
- career breaks
- flexible working patterns
- the right to request flexible working.

The Government is working hard to promote the concept of work-life balance and many organisations are beginning to embrace it. Family-friendly policies represent the mainstream of this initiative. However, it is useful to see how they fit into the wider context of the work-life balance and the following section aims to give this perspective. For example, much of what is said about the implementation of a work-life balance strategy is equally applicable to family-friendly policies and the introduction of flexible working practices.

Work-life Balance

Many employees struggle, and often fail, to juggle long working hours with their family responsibilities, due largely to the emphasis placed by many employers on quantity of hours, rather than quality of work. Many employees are then forced into making an unwelcome choice between dedication to their job in order to achieve career success (ie working long hours) and commitment and loyalty to their family (ie maintaining a reasonable balance between working hours and family responsibilities).

It is still common for employees' commitment to their work to be measured in terms of the number of hours they work, rather than in terms of their work output, quality or value to the organisation. This is despite the fact that it is well known that more hours do not necessarily result in higher quality work; indeed the opposite effect is frequently achieved.

Instead of insisting on long working hours, employers should aim to:
- review the culture of working hours and working patterns within their organisation, and be prepared to work towards changing them
- consider conducting a confidential attitude survey as a starting point towards reviewing working hours and patterns of working
- assess ways of allowing employees who work long hours to reduce their hours, for example by recruiting additional staff, redistributing workloads or re-structuring jobs
- understand that working long hours can be detrimental to both the employee and the employer in the long run
- consider alternative ways of working, such as job-sharing, flexible working hours and term-time working (see Chapter 9)
- adopt a positive approach and seek to adapt existing working hours requirements (where possible) to accommodate employees' personal needs.

The Department of Trade and Industry (DTI) published a consultation document titled *Work and Families, Choice and Flexibilities* in February 2005. In this document, the DTI commented that employers have an important role to play in supporting family-friendly working practices, and published a set of proposals aimed at providing more choices for employees with families as to how they might balance their work and caring responsibilities. Amongst the key principles of the consultation was the aim of responding to the changing patterns of employment by ensuring that parents and others with caring responsibilities have genuine choices about how they balance work and family life. The results of the consultation, which are available at *www.dti.gov.uk*, formed the basis of legislative measures to enhance employees' maternity, adoption and paternity rights as from April 2007.

According to the DTI in 2004, on the issue of work-life balance:

- almost one-fifth (19%) of employees would like to be able to work part time, the same number for those with caring responsibilities
- slightly more (21%) would like to work annualised hours (having to work a certain number of hours each year but being able to vary the number of hours worked at different times of the year), the same number for people with caring responsibilities
- around 12% of employees would like the option of a job-share; this is 19% for people with caring responsibilities
- more than one-third (34%) of employees would like the opportunity to work flexitime, compared with 37% for people with caring responsibilities
- the same number (34%) would like to work compressed hours (for example, allowing an employee to do a full-time job in four days a week instead of five); this figure is 37% for those with caring responsibilities
- over a quarter (26%) would like to be able to work from home, only 1% less than the figure for those with caring responsibilities.

On flexible working practices in both the private and public sectors, the research found that:

- almost a quarter (24%) of all employees currently work flexitime, although 35% of employees want to
- almost 1 in 6 employees (17%) say that flexitime is compatible with the work they do but do not think their employer would allow them to work flexitime
- only 6% of employees currently work a compressed working week but 33% would like to do so
- around 14% of employees say that working compressed hours is compatible with the work they do but do not think they would be allowed by their employer to work this way.

The following advice comes from *Creating a Work-Life Balance — a good practice guide for employers*, published in September 2000 by the then Department for Education and Employment (DfEE), now the Department for Education and Skills (DfES).

1. Look at the need.
- Survey staff about how they would like to balance work and their private lives.

- Involve staff associations and/or trade unions in the development of surveys.
- Work out what the organisation wants: eg, improved recruitment and retention; modernised employment practices in line with the business need; increased motivation and loyalty among employees; better productivity and reduced absenteeism; reduced stress, producing better-focused staff.

2. Formulate policies.

- Consult widely.
- Agree strategies.
- Construct written procedures for implementation and monitoring the policies.
- Test a new idea against the organisation's criteria and against what staff say. For example, will it: attract new employees, help retain staff, build diversity in skills and personnel, balance staffing levels more effectively, improve morale, reduce sickness and absenteeism, enhance working relationships between colleagues, involve reorganising responsibilities, require changes in supervision or management?
- Produce a business case.

3. Communicate change.

- Get management on board — educate and train middle managers in the benefits of implementing work-life balance policies.
- Cascade policies — consider using workshops, role play, newsletters, leaflets, notice boards, appraisals.

4. Run a pilot or trial period and evaluate it.

5. Amend the programme, if necessary, and extend it, if needed.

6. Follow up.

- Monitor and evaluate to check the programme is working.
- Consider the use of questionnaires and appraisals.
- Be prepared to adjust the programme as the need arises.
- Maintain an open-door policy to listen to staff.
- Continue a two-way communication process.

Many employers are experiencing considerable benefits as a result of introducing one or more of these options, including:

- attracting the best talent
- retaining valued staff
- improving productivity and performance
- increasing morale, commitment and loyalty
- reducing absenteeism, sickness and stress.

For a work-life balance strategy to be really successful, it must be built on a solid business case linked to the organisation's objectives and business plan. Employers need to identify core business needs and then tailor policies to suit both operational and employee needs.

THE BUSINESS CASE

Some employers, while recognising the need for adopting family-friendly policies, are still very wary of this more flexible approach to working practices even though there are plenty of examples of organisations where introducing such initiatives has improved productivity and helped businesses to succeed. The business case for providing the flexibility for different ways of working is a strong one.

In a Factsheet (titled "Work-Life Balance") revised and published in June 2006, the Chartered Institute of Personnel and Development (CIPD) suggests that all employers should take an interest in work-life balance because in today's 24-hour, 7-day society, more and more people need to juggle responsibilities between home and work.

The Factsheet points out that employers' ambitions to have a high-performing organisation and a highly motivated workforce, and employees' desires to have working arrangements that suit their personal commitments (rather than having to put up with overwork and excessive hours) do not present a conflict of interest. CIPD research shows that these can be powerful complementary rather than conflicting forces.

The CIPD suggests that employers should consider not only the needs of employees who are parents of young children, as this approach can alienate employees with other family responsibilities, for example the several million people in Britain who have caring responsibilities for elderly or disabled relatives or friends. The Factsheet further points out that many employees with no dependants may have commitments within the community or might reasonably want time to pursue personal interests such as travel, study or leisure activities.

The Factsheet states the business case for work-life balance clearly and coherently, listing the following benefits to business that can be attained:
- higher productivity and competitiveness
- increased flexibility and customer service, for example to cover for absence and holidays
- raised morale, motivation, commitment and engagement

- reduced absenteeism
- improved recruitment and retention of a diverse workforce
- the opportunity to become an employer of choice
- meeting legal requirements.

The Factsheet states that, although employers may incur costs in adopting policies to support work-life balance, including increased managerial workloads, these costs are generally outweighed by the gains. It points out that the biggest obstacle to implementing policies that support work-life balance is line manager attitude and resistance. Such negative attitudes are often based on assumptions about the problems that flexible working will cause, which usually turn out to be unfounded.

The Factsheet goes on to suggest that there is no one type of flexible work-life balance policy that suits all employers and provides a non-exhaustive list of practices that employers might want to consider adopting. The list includes:

- part-time working and job-sharing
- flexible start/finish times
- working from home
- term-time working
- annualised hours
- nine-day fortnight
- extended leave and other time off arrangements such as career breaks, sabbaticals and study leave.

As far as actions are concerned, the CIPD recommends that employers should:

- identify their business needs, so as to demonstrate to colleagues how a work-life balance strategy will benefit both the business and the workforce as a whole
- adopt policies to match their operational needs by examining both business and employee priorities and considering any potential impact on customers
- include measures for performance that are based on outcomes and results, rather than on presence at the workplace
- develop clear management guidelines to facilitate fair treatment and help to gain line managers' commitment
- lead from the top by identifying a senior management champion and/or senior management role models who are actively practising work-life balance

- communicate the organisation's plans using a wide variety of media to involve employees
- monitor progress and draw lessons from the experience.

The CIPD Factsheet is available at *www.cipd.co.uk*.

Some of the key benefits of flexible working practices, and the rationale behind them, are explored further below.

Attracting the Best Talent

Skilled people have more choices than ever before about where to work and for whom. Furthermore it is becoming less and less common for employees to remain with the same employer for long periods of time. British employers are not just competing with others in the UK for talent. They now face global competition.

Family-friendly policies are a recruitment tool, enabling employers to attract the best talent. Improved recruitment is without doubt one of the main benefits recognised by employers who offer family-friendly policies. Offering more flexible working arrangements attracts a wider range of candidates for vacancies, including older workers, people wishing to work part time and those with caring responsibilities who may need a pattern of working that is flexible enough to fit in with the needs of their families. People with disabilities or health problems can also gain improved access to work. Thus, employers who offer flexible working arrangements are maximising the availability of labour. For example, by offering a job-share, the employer is widening out the pool of available applicants to embrace talented individuals who cannot, or do not wish to, work full time.

There is also plenty of evidence to suggest that younger workers make choices about whom they want to work for based on criteria other than financial rewards. Fast-track graduates and talented people with experience alike may well be prepared to join an organisation offering a better quality of life rather than a higher salary.

Retaining Valued Staff

The high cost, both in terms of time and money, of recruiting and training new employees makes retention of existing staff vital. Typical recruitment costs in 2006 of replacing an individual have been estimated by the Chartered Institute of Personnel and Development (CIPD) at around £3600. For managerial or professional staff, the cost was found to be in excess of £5000. If, however, the "add-on" costs, such as time spent drafting job descriptions and person specifications, personnel administration and induction are taken into account, the average cost is around £8200. Staff who leave walk away with valuable experience and job knowledge that is difficult and costly to replace.

Family-friendly policies are closely linked to staff retention and staff retention is in turn related to customer satisfaction. Employees dealing with customers over a period of time anticipate their needs and are more effective. In turn, when customers recognise the staff who serve them and build up a rapport, they are far more likely to return. In this way employee retention can be a key driver of customer retention.

Improving Productivity and Performance

UK employers operate in an increasingly competitive environment in which flexibility is key to meeting customer demands. Flexibility helps a wide range of businesses respond to changing market conditions. It helps service sector organisations to meet customers' expectations of services being available around the clock. It also enables those working globally to cover American and Far Eastern working times.

Employees at all stages of their lives are most productive if they are able to achieve an appropriate balance between work and other aspects of their lives, thereby facilitating enhanced delivery of organisational objectives. For example, employers who facilitate job-sharing invariably report that they gain a great deal from the arrangement. They say that, more often than not, they are getting one and a half employees for the cost of one.

In a performance-based culture, businesses are under pressure to embrace change and keep up with the competition. Employees who have young children or other caring commitments have different needs, with a greater emphasis on their interaction with the family. Family-friendly policies and the associated flexibility engender an overall ability to adapt to the changing needs of business.

Increasing Morale, Commitment and Loyalty

Experience has shown that when employers truly and actively engage in policies that benefit people, the degree of engagement and commitment to that organisation is greatly increased. Research has shown that family-friendly policies increase motivation, morale and loyalty. Again, employee loyalty is related to customer loyalty, which in turn contributes to an organisation's growth and success. Furthermore, some organisations have found that when the focus is on the task rather than the time spent doing it and individuals are trusted to do their jobs to the best of their ability, their commitment is reciprocated. For example, where an employer is flexible and changes a start time to allow a parent to drop children at school or allows home working to accommodate eldercare needs, this is rewarded in improved morale, commitment and loyalty.

Reducing Absenteeism, Sickness and Stress

Enabling employees to integrate caring responsibilities into their daily lives, without detriment to their work or home, will result in marked reductions in stress levels, sickness and absenteeism. This will also have a beneficial impact on relationships at work with colleagues and customers alike. A reduction in stress levels will result in better performance for the business. Working conditions such as the long hours culture restrict the potential of many employees and results in stress and reduced effectiveness. Family-friendly policies and their associated flexibility in working patterns allow employees to look after their dependants in their own time rather than the employer's time.

Gaining a Reputation as a Good Employer

Employers that are seen to operate practices leading to a reasonable work-life balance for their employees receive considerable positive PR. The ability of an organisation to reflect its stakeholders in its employee diversity adds another opportunity to become not only an employer of choice but also an organisation with whom others choose to do business. Having a wide range of employees enables organisations to understand and reflect diverse and global customers better.

CHAPTER 2

MATERNITY POLICIES, LEAVE AND ASSOCIATED ISSUES

INTRODUCTION

Statistics demonstrate that there is an increasing number of women who wish to return to work following the birth of a child. Many choose to do so on a full-time basis, but many others seek to negotiate a different, more family-friendly working pattern, for example part-time working or with flexibility in working hours.

According to research published by the Government in 2006, 80 per cent of women who took maternity leave in 2005 returned to work afterwards, whilst three quarters of returners went back on a part-time basis (*Maternity and Paternity Rights and Benefits: Survey of Parents 2005*, available at *www.dti.gov.uk*).

This chapter explores the rights of employees who are pregnant and who take maternity leave, including rights during and at the end of maternity leave.

The rights discussed in this chapter apply only to employees, ie those engaged by the employer under a contract of employment. Other workers, for example casual staff, freelance workers and sub-contractors, have no entitlements.

LEGAL REQUIREMENTS — A SUMMARY

Employees who become pregnant enjoy considerable protection and benefits under various statutes. These include:

- the right to time off work for antenatal care
- the right to paid suspension from work in certain circumstances in order to protect the employee's health and safety
- the right to take maternity leave and resume working afterwards
- the right (subject to the employer's agreement) to work for up to ten days during maternity leave without bringing the leave period to an end and without any loss of statutory maternity pay
- the right to receive statutory maternity pay (subject to a minimum of six months' service)
- protection from detriment and dismissal for a reason related to pregnancy, childbirth or maternity leave.

TIME OFF FOR ANTENATAL CARE

An employee who is pregnant and has made an appointment to receive antenatal care on the advice of a registered medical practitioner, registered midwife or registered health worker, has the statutory right to take a reasonable amount of time off with pay to keep the appointment. The employer must not unreasonably refuse a request for time off, but may request evidence that an appointment has been made (see below).

The right to time off for antenatal care applies to all pregnant employees; it does not depend upon the number of hours worked or length of service. An employee who is taking time off is entitled to be paid for the absence at her appropriate hourly rate of pay.

Employers are not entitled to require an employee to rearrange her working days or hours to accommodate antenatal appointments, nor to make up for lost time by working additional hours. The employee's right is to take time off out of normal working hours and to be paid normal pay for those hours.

Legislation does not define antenatal care other than by stating that it must be on the advice of a registered medical practitioner, midwife or health visitor. It would be difficult categorically to define what is meant by antenatal care since obviously it may vary, depending upon the general state of health of the particular employee.

How Much Time Off?

The right to time off during working hours is qualified by a condition of reasonableness. An employee should not be unreasonably refused time off work for the purpose of receiving antenatal care. Though the law anticipates certain instances when it would be reasonable for the employer to refuse to give a pregnant employee paid time off, it is not particularly helpful, since no guidance is given as to how an employer should determine what is reasonable or unreasonable.

As a general rule, tribunals are reluctant to find that a refusal is reasonable when medical advisors have recommended that an appointment be made. A tribunal would, however, base its decision on the merits of each individual case. For example, in the case of part-time staff and shift workers, it may be arguable that for attendance at non-urgent antenatal classes and/or relaxation classes, an employer may not be acting unreasonably in refusing paid time off if an employee could reasonably arrange the appointments outside her normal working hours. Of course, in practice, the timing of appointments is generally outside the individual's control and so it may not always be possible for the employee to arrange an appointment outside her normal working hours. Nevertheless, if an employee refuses to co-operate with a request to arrange appointments outside working hours without good reason, it may be perfectly within the employer's right to refuse her paid time off. An employee is expected to comply with such a request as far as possible and if unable to do so she should be able to justify this to her employer.

Evidence of the Appointment

An employer is entitled to ask an employee who requests time off for antenatal care to provide evidence of the appointment (except for the first appointment) and to produce a certificate stating that she is pregnant from a registered medical practitioner, a registered midwife or a registered health visitor. If an employee fails to provide the employer with the above on request, then the employer is not required to permit the employee to take paid time off to keep the antenatal appointment.

Remedies

If an employer has unreasonably refused to allow an employee to take time off for antenatal care or has failed to pay the whole or part of her pay during such time off, she may bring a complaint to an employment tribunal. The complaint must be presented within three months of the date of the particular appointment, although the tribunal has discretion to extend the time limit for such further period as it considers reasonable, if it is of the view that it was not reasonably practicable for the employee to bring the case within this time period.

Where the tribunal upholds a complaint it must make a declaration to that effect and order the employer to pay the amount due to the employee or the amount to which she would have been entitled had the time off not been refused.

RIGHTS TO PAID SUSPENSION FROM WORK ON HEALTH AND SAFETY GROUNDS

There are a number of health and safety provisions in place for the protection of pregnant women at work contained in the **Employment Rights Act 1996** and the **Management of Health and Safety at Work Regulations 1999**. Specifically, employers must not permit a pregnant or breastfeeding woman to continue working in her normal job if to do so would place her at risk of harm to her health or that of her baby. A risk might arise from the employee's working conditions, work processes or specific job duties.

It is important to note that the health and safety provisions that protect pregnant employees in this way apply where a pregnant employee's health or safety could be placed at risk on account of her job or working conditions. They do not come into play in circumstances where a pregnant employee falls ill or is signed off work by her doctor.

If risks to a pregnant woman are identified, whether as a result of a risk assessment, a recommendation by the employee's doctor or by the employee herself raising a matter of concern, the employer must alter the employee's working conditions in order to remove her from exposure to the risk in question. If the employee is employed on night work, the employer must adjust her hours of work if she produces a certificate from her doctor recommending that she should not work at night.

If it is not possible for the employer to alter the employee's working conditions (or in the case of a night worker, the hours of work), the next course of action the employer must consider in order to protect the employee is a temporary transfer to a different job. The employer is not obliged to create a special job for an employee in these circumstances, but rather is obliged to offer her any suitable alternative job that exists.

Where such a transfer is offered, the employer must ensure that the work is suitable. "Suitable" in this context means work which is appropriate for the employee to do in the circumstances, and which is on terms and conditions not substantially less favourable than those of her normal job.

If despite the employer's best efforts, no suitable alternative work can be identified, then the employer must suspend the employee from work on full pay until the commencement of her maternity leave.

This provision is mandatory. The employee may complain to an employment tribunal if her employer has failed to offer her suitable alternative work (where such is available), or has refused to pay her all or part of the remuneration to which she is entitled.

MATERNITY LEAVE

Maternity leave lasting 52 weeks is available to all pregnant employees, irrespective of length of service, number of hours worked, age or marital status.

The first 26 weeks of maternity leave is known as "ordinary maternity leave", whilst the second period of 26 weeks is called "additional maternity leave". Additional maternity leave begins on the day after ordinary maternity leave ends. The distinction between the two periods of leave remains in place essentially because different terms and conditions apply during each.

No woman is allowed to return to work during the first two weeks after giving birth. This is known as the "compulsory maternity leave period". Any employer who allows a woman to return to work during this period is committing a criminal offence and could be fined. For factory work, the rules are stricter — women must not return within four weeks of giving birth.

Notification Requirements

By the end of the "qualifying week", ie the 15th week before the baby is due (unless this is not reasonably practicable) the pregnant employee must notify the employer of the following:
- the fact that she is pregnant
- her expected week of childbirth (the employer may ask to see a certificate from a doctor or midwife to confirm this)
- the date she intends to start her leave (this must be in writing if the employer requests it).

"Childbirth" means the birth of a living child or the birth of a child, whether living or dead, after 24 weeks of pregnancy.

"Expected week of childbirth" means the week, beginning with midnight between Saturday and Sunday, in which it is expected that the child will be born.

Notification of Change of Start Date

A pregnant employee is entitled to change the date when she intends to start her maternity leave, providing she:

- gives her employer at least 28 days' notice of the new date, whether it falls earlier or later than the original notified date
- puts the request in writing, if the employer requests it.

If it is not reasonably practicable for the woman to give 28 days' notice of the change, then she must notify the employer as soon as she can.

Responding to an Employee's Notification

When an employer receives notice from an employee that she intends to go on maternity leave, it must respond within 28 days. This reply must inform the employee of the date on which her maternity leave will end, calculated in accordance with her chosen start date. The date will be the date that falls 52 weeks after the chosen start date. Where the employee subsequently changes her mind about when to start her maternity leave, then the deadline for writing to tell her when she is due to return will be within 28 days from the date she notified the new date.

An employer who does not write to the employee within the 28-day period loses the right to prevent her returning to work before the end of her maternity leave period without giving notice, or to dismiss or discipline the employee for returning to work after the due return date.

Timing of Maternity Leave

The employee may not start her leave before the 11th week before the expected week of childbirth (EWC) unless the baby is born before then. If the baby is born before the employee had intended to start her maternity leave, then she must inform the employer as soon as possible, giving the date of birth and, if she has not already done so, a certificate showing when the child was originally expected.

Apart from the above restrictions, the employee has the freedom to choose when to begin her maternity leave and the employer may not require her to start her leave earlier or later than she wishes. If, however, she is absent from work for a pregnancy-related reason after the beginning of the fourth week before her expected week of childbirth, then her maternity leave is triggered automatically.

STATUTORY MATERNITY PAY

During maternity leave, the employee's normal wages or salary are not payable, but she will be entitled to receive statutory maternity pay (SMP) for the first 39 weeks of maternity leave provided she meets certain qualifying conditions.

1. She must have been employed continuously for at least 26 weeks by the end of the qualifying week.
2. She must have average weekly earnings in the qualifying period (which is the period of eight weeks running into the qualifying week) above the lower earnings limit for National Insurance purposes (£84 per week — £87 per week from 1 April 2007).
3. She must still be pregnant at the 11th week before the baby is due, or have had the baby by then, due to a premature birth.
4. She must have stopped working for the employer.

If an employee is ineligible to receive statutory maternity pay, this will not affect her right to take maternity leave — which will then be unpaid — or her right to resume working after the birth of her child.

Payment of Statutory Maternity Pay

SMP is paid for 39 weeks of the employee's maternity leave (known as the "maternity pay period"). It is payable by the employer, provided the employee is eligible, whether or not the employee intends to return to work. The employer may make the payment for less than 39 weeks if the employee:

- returns to work before the end of her maternity leave (except on "keeping in touch days" (see below))
- starts work after the birth with a new employer who is not liable to pay the statutory maternity pay
- dies
- is taken into legal custody.

Payment of SMP cannot begin before the employee starts her maternity leave nor earlier than the 11th week before the expected week of childbirth, unless the baby is born prematurely. SMP can start on any day of the week.

The Government has stated an intention to extend statutory maternity pay to 52 weeks by the end of the current parliament. When this occurs, employees who qualify will be entitled to receive SMP throughout the whole of their period of maternity leave.

Rates of Statutory Maternity Pay

SMP is paid at two rates.
1. The higher rate — 90% of the employee's average weekly earnings — is payable for the first six weeks of maternity leave.
2. The lower rate is a fixed weekly rate set each year, which currently stands at the lower of £108.85 (£112.75 per week from 1 April 2007) or 90% of the employee's average weekly earnings, and is payable for the remaining 33 weeks.

SMP is part of gross pay and is subject to deductions for PAYE, tax and National Insurance contributions in the usual way.

Calculation of Statutory Maternity Pay

An employee's eligibility for SMP and the amount payable during the first six weeks of maternity leave stand to be based on her average weekly earnings over the period of eight weeks that run up to and including the qualifying week. Any pay rise, including a pay rise that is introduced later on and backdated to the eight-week reference period, must be included in this calculation.

Furthermore, following the case of *Alabaster v Woolwich plc & another* [2004] IRLR 486 ECJ, C-147/02, employers must recalculate an employee's SMP in circumstances where a pay rise is implemented at any time between the beginning of the eight-week reference period and the end of her maternity leave, whether backdated or not. This means, for example, that SMP paid to the employee during the first six weeks of her maternity leave (at the rate of 90% of her normal earnings) would have to be recalculated so as to factor in the pay increase in retrospect, with the difference between the amount of SMP already paid in respect of the six-week period and the new amount due being paid to the employee.

Recovery of Statutory Maternity Pay

All employers can recover SMP paid to employees. Most employers can recover 92% of the sums paid. Small employers can recover 100% of statutory maternity pay, plus 4.5% National Insurance compensation.

To be classified as a small employer, the gross National Insurance contributions of the business (employees and employers) in the last qualifying tax year must be less than £45,000.

The qualifying tax year is the last completed tax year before the pregnant employee's qualifying week.

The recovery is made by deducting the relevant amount from the gross National Insurance element of the monthly payroll payment due to the Collector of Taxes. If there is insufficient National Insurance to cover this, a deduction can be made from the PAYE element of the remittance.

Medical Evidence for Statutory Maternity Pay

An employer can refuse to pay SMP if medical evidence (usually on a form MAT B1) is not produced by the third week of the maternity pay period.

Records for Statutory Maternity Pay

All employers must, by law, keep the following records for at least three years following the end of the tax year to which they relate:
- all medical evidence, eg MAT B1 forms
- copies of any medical evidence if the original documents have been returned to the employee
- dates of the maternity leave notified by the employee
- details of weeks within the maternity pay period for which SMP was paid and the amounts
- details of weeks within the maternity pay period when SMP was not paid and the reasons.

EMPLOYEES' RIGHTS DURING MATERNITY LEAVE

A employee's contract of employment continues throughout both ordinary and additional maternity leave.

Rights and Duties during Ordinary Maternity Leave

During ordinary maternity leave, the employee must continue to benefit from all her terms and conditions of employment, except remuneration. Most employees will be entitled to SMP and some organisations give their female staff contractual maternity pay, ie continue full or part salary/wages through all or part of maternity leave.

While absent on ordinary maternity leave, employees continue to be bound by any obligations arising from their terms and conditions of employment.

Rights and Duties during Additional Maternity Leave

During additional maternity leave the situation is different. The law requires that the terms relating to notice of termination, redundancy pay and disciplinary and grievance procedures must apply. Furthermore, mutual trust and confidence continues to apply. The position as regards an employee's entitlement to accrue statutory annual holiday during additional maternity leave is, at present, not clear. To be safe, employers should assume that statutory annual holiday will continue to accrue during additional maternity leave, as well as during ordinary maternity leave. All other terms and conditions of employment may, however, be suspended during additional maternity leave. Nevertheless, if the employer intends to withdraw any contractual benefits during additional maternity leave, this should be set out in its policies and procedures. When deciding this matter, it is advisable to consider whether those benefits would be withdrawn during other sorts of extended leave. If not, then the employer could be vulnerable to a sex discrimination claim.

An employee on additional maternity leave remains bound by the implied obligation of good faith to her employer and any terms relating to notice, disclosure of confidential information, acceptance of gifts or other benefits and participation in any other business.

Keeping in Touch Days

A new provision permitting "keeping in touch days" was introduced in respect of employees whose child was expected to be born on or after 1 April 2007. This provision allows a woman on maternity leave to go into work for up to ten days (which may be either separate days or a single block) without losing any statutory maternity pay or triggering the end of her maternity leave. For this provision to operate, both the employer and the employee must agree:

- that the employee will do some work
- the type of work, for example attendance at a training course
- the amount of remuneration that will be payable in respect of the work done (the employer can offset the SMP paid in respect of the working days against wages/salary).

This provision does not allow an employer to insist that an employee on maternity leave should come in to work, nor does it confer a right on the employee to be offered any work.

Reasonable Contact

Over and above the "keeping in touch days" discussed above, employers may maintain reasonable contact with employees on maternity leave. This may, for example, be in order to discuss the employee's plans for returning to work or to provide her with an update on developments in the workplace.

Maternity and Redundancy

If an employee's job becomes redundant during her ordinary or additional maternity leave, she is entitled to be offered a suitable alternative vacancy if there is one available. If there is a suitable job and the employee is made redundant without being offered it, her dismissal will be unfair. This is the case irrespective of whether the employee is ready to return to work at the relevant time. A claim for sex discrimination would also be likely to succeed in these circumstances.

RIGHT TO RETURN TO WORK

Notification Periods

If a woman decides to take the full period of maternity leave to which she is entitled, she need not give her employer any prior notice of her return date. She may simply return on the first working day after her full entitlement to leave has ended, in accordance with the date notified to her by the employer.

If, however, the employee wishes to return to work before the end of her maternity leave, she must give her employer at least eight weeks' notice of her intended return date. If she attempts to come back to work without having done this, then the employer may postpone her return to a date that will provide eight weeks' notice. The employer may not, however, use this provision to postpone the employee's return beyond the date when her maternity leave was due to end anyway.

If the employer has not given the employee proper notice of when she was due to return to work in the first place, the employee cannot be prevented from coming back early, even if she has not given the correct notice.

Apart from the provisions noted above, there are no other circumstances in which it is lawful for either the employer or the employee to postpone the employee's return to work beyond the end of her statutory maternity leave.

Sickness at the End of Maternity Leave

If the employee cannot return to work at the end of her maternity leave because she is ill, she should notify the employer in accordance with the normal company rules relating to sickness absence. If she qualifies, she should be paid statutory sick pay (SSP) and/or company sick pay in the normal way. In effect, the day on which she should have returned will be the first day in a period of sickness absence.

Resignation

If a woman decides not to return from maternity leave at all, then she must give her employer notice of her resignation in accordance with the terms of her contract. Her employment will then come to an end at the end of her notice period. This will not affect her entitlement to SMP.

Rights on Return from Ordinary Maternity Leave

When an employee returns to work from ordinary maternity leave, she is entitled to return to the same job she was in before she went on leave, on terms and conditions that are no less favourable than those which would have applied if she had not been absent. Seniority and other similar rights must also be the same as they would have been if she had not been absent.

"Job" in this context means the nature of the work which the employee is employed to do in accordance with her contract and the capacity and place in which she is so employed.

Rights on Return from Additional Maternity Leave

When an employee returns from additional maternity leave, she is entitled to return to her old job unless the employer can show that it was not reasonably practicable for her to do so. In these circumstances, she must be offered another job that is suitable and appropriate for her to do and which is on terms and conditions that are no less favourable than those that would have applied if she had not gone on leave. Where employment rights depend on seniority, the woman's employment before going on leave should be treated as continuous with her employment after coming back to work.

If there has been a general pay rise during the employee's maternity leave, her wages/salary should be increased accordingly on her return.

Return to Work Part Time

Many women seek to return to work on a part-time basis following maternity leave. This is inconsistent with the statutory right, which is to return to the same job. Where, however, an employer refuses to allow a woman to return on a part-time basis and she consequently declines to return (or reluctantly returns on a full-time basis), the woman may bring a complaint of indirect sex discrimination (see **Sex Discrimination Act 1975**) against her employer in an employment tribunal. The logic of such a complaint is that:

- the employer has applied a provision that the employee must work full-time
- this requirement has a disproportionate adverse impact on women compared with men because more women than men have the prime responsibility for the care of young children
- if the employee can show that the employer's insistence on full-time working was to her detriment, the employee will succeed in her complaint unless the employer cannot justify refusing part-time working on objective grounds in her particular case.

Over and above the possibility of a claim for indirect sex discrimination, an employee in these circumstance may lodge a request for flexible working which the employer would be obliged to consider seriously through a prescribed procedure (see Chapter 10).

TEMPORARY REPLACEMENTS

If a temporary replacement is recruited to replace an employee on maternity leave, the replacement will technically be engaged on a fixed-term contract terminable on the occurrence of the original employee's return to work. Thus the temporary replacement will be protected by the provisions of the **Fixed-term Employees (Prevention of Less Favourable Treatment) Regulations 2002**, which require employers not to treat fixed-term employees less favourably than comparable permanent employees unless there is an objective reason for any less favourable treatment.

Dismissing a temporary replacement on the return to work of the original employee is potentially fair, but is nevertheless subject to all the usual unfair dismissal rules. The reason for dismissal will be the return to work of the employee who has been on maternity leave and this will be a sufficiently substantial reason to justify the dismissal as fair, provided that:

- the temporary replacement employee was notified on engagement that his/her employment would terminate on the employee's return from maternity leave
- as much warning as possible is given of the likely date of dismissal
- the employer seeks to establish whether alternative work is available for the temporary employee on the return to work of the original employee
- the employer follows the three stages of the statutory dismissal and disciplinary procedure (DDP), namely notifies the employee in writing of the circumstances likely to lead to termination, holds a meeting with him/her to discuss the circumstances (including whether any alternative work is available) and allows a right of appeal against a decision to dismiss.

PROTECTION FROM DETRIMENT AND DISMISSAL

If an employee is subjected to any unfavourable treatment at work for a reason related to the fact she is pregnant or because she has taken maternity leave, she may complain to an employment tribunal. The law protects her from detrimental treatment on such grounds.

Similarly, if an employee is dismissed for any reason connected with pregnancy or childbirth, or for taking maternity leave, the dismissal will be automatically unfair. No qualifying service is needed to claim unfair dismissal in such circumstances. Furthermore, a claim for sex discrimination would be very likely to succeed.

CONTINUITY OF SERVICE

Once an employee has returned to work following ordinary or additional maternity leave, all periods of maternity leave must be counted as continuous service for the purpose of the employee's statutory rights. This means that if at some future date it becomes necessary for statutory reasons to calculate the employee's total length of service (for example, if she is made redundant), this must be calculated to include the whole of the period during which she was absent from work on maternity leave.

The position with an employee's contractual rights is slightly different. During ordinary maternity leave, all contractual rights except for remuneration continue and it follows that the period of ordinary maternity leave must count towards the employee's seniority in this respect. This is also the case during any period of additional maternity leave in which the employer chooses to pay the employee all or part of her wage or salary. In contrast, a period of additional maternity leave that is *unpaid* need not be counted in respect of the employee's seniority, pension rights and other similar contractual rights. In this case, the employee's right will be to have her total length of service calculated as if the two periods either side of the period of unpaid additional maternity leave had been continuous with each other.

FUTURE DEVELOPMENTS

At the time of writing, the Government has announced that it plans to:
- increase paid maternity leave from the current 39 weeks to 52 weeks
- make some of maternity leave transferable from the mother to the father.

It is expected that these two provisions will be introduced at the same time.

In respect of the second provision, the proposal is to introduce a new statutory right to 26 weeks additional paternity leave and additional paternity pay for the employee's husband/partner during the second six months of the employee's maternity leave, provided the employee has returned to work. Fathers will, if eligible, be able to take additional paternity leave once the child is at least 20 weeks old and the period of leave will have to be complete by the child's first birthday. If the employee, at the time of her return to work, has some of her entitlement to SMP left, the father will be entitled to be paid an equivalent amount of SPP (statutory paternity pay) whilst on leave.

DEVISING A MATERNITY POLICY

Employers should draw up and implement a maternity policy and procedure, taking into account the following points. This will ensure that everyone receives fair and consistent treatment.

Who Will be Responsible for Notifying a Pregnant Employee of Her Rights?

The HR department or the employee's line manager should be given responsibility for notifying a pregnant employee of her rights. Although there is no statutory obligation to inform an employee of her rights, it is likely that any organisation wanting to draw up a maternity policy would see this as an integral part of it.

Health and Safety Considerations

There is no obligation on an employee to tell her employer that she is pregnant (unless she wants time off for antenatal care) until the qualifying week (ie the 15th week before the expected week of childbirth), at which time she must give notice of the date on which she wishes to start her maternity leave. An exception to this might arise where there are particular health and safety considerations. Employers who think that their female employees might be put at risk (perhaps because a substance with which they normally work quite safely is potentially harmful to an unborn child), should do all they reasonably can to eliminate the risk or, if this is not possible, warn employees of the dangers and impress on them the importance of notifying the organisation as soon as they think they might be pregnant. The employee's health and safety at work is the employer's responsibility.

Notifying the Employer

The employer should consider how pregnant employees should be required to notify them of their pregnancy, or give notice of going on maternity leave. For example, a specific form might be used which would need to state to whom the notification should be given.

Payment of Statutory Maternity Pay

An employee who is excluded from receiving statutory maternity pay (SMP) must be given a written statement setting out the reasons for this. Ideally form SMP1 should be used. To be on the safe side, employers should accept only the maternity certificate (form Mat Bl) as evidence of the expected week of childbirth. This cannot be issued until the employee is at least 26 weeks' pregnant. Until that time other evidence of the expected week of childbirth will be available, from which the employee's likely entitlement can be assessed, but SMP should not be paid until the Mat Bl has been received. There are no hard and fast rules as to how SMP must be paid (ie in a lump sum, at the normal pay interval, etc). The employer's procedure in this respect should be clearly set down.

Rights During Maternity Leave

The employee's rights and position during both types of maternity leave should be set down in writing. If this is not done, it is all too easy to grant contractual rights to an employee unintentionally. Setting down the employer's view of the situation in writing should avoid this problem. Provision should be made as to the status of the contract, making it clear that during both types of maternity leave the employment contract will remain in force. The position on contractual benefits and other perks during additional maternity leave should also be made clear.

Problems frequently arise over issues such as the return of a company car. The employer has to maintain all contractual benefits throughout ordinary maternity leave such as use of a company car, luncheon vouchers, etc. During additional maternity leave, the position is different and the employer may elect to withdraw such contractual benefits. The employer should therefore make clear whether these contractual benefits will be continued or withdrawn. If it is the employer's policy or practice to continue contractual benefits during other types of extended absence (for example, sickness absence), it may be vulnerable to a sex discrimination claim if benefits are withdrawn during additional maternity leave.

Establishing the Date of Childbirth

It is necessary to obtain the actual date of childbirth as soon as is reasonably practicable. Apart from statutory reasons, the employer may wish to send flowers or notify colleagues. The employee must not be allowed to return to work (or do any work at home) during the two week period of compulsory maternity leave which commences with the date that the birth occurs. In addition, it is illegal to employ a woman to do manual work in a factory or workplace within four weeks of giving birth.

Establishing the Employee's Intentions as Regards Her Return

An employee is not required to notify her employer of her intention to return from maternity leave unless she wishes to return early. If she does wish to return early, the employee must give eight weeks notice. If she fails to give the requisite eight weeks notice, the employer is entitled to postpone her return so that the employer has the benefit of the full eight weeks notice. However, the employer cannot use this provision to postpone the return beyond the end of the relevant period of maternity leave. There are no other provisions for postponing the return from maternity leave. Confirmation of the employee's restart details (ie return date, contractual rights and benefits, job details, etc) should be sent to her once the notified date of return has been confirmed. If a woman cannot return to work because she is ill, then the normal company rules on sick leave will apply.

Same Job, Same Rights

The employee's right to return from a period of ordinary maternity leave is a right to return to the job in which she was employed before her absence with her seniority and other rights as they would have been had she not been absent, and on terms and conditions no less favourable than those that would have applied if she had not been absent.

An employee who has taken additional maternity leave is entitled to return to the same job. "Job" is defined as the nature of the work which she is employed to do in accordance with her contract and the capacity and place in which she is so employed. This is not necessarily exactly what she was doing prior to her maternity leave; for example, it is not necessarily the right to return to the same desk in the same room doing exactly the same work as before. For example, if the employee was employed as a secretary she may be required to return to any secretarial post of the same status, on the same terms and conditions. However, if her job was "secretary to the finance director", she must return to that job. Or, if an employee was employed as "accountant in the finance division" and on her return she had to work for a different person on different accounts in the same division, there would be no breach of her right to return. It is all a question of what is contained in the contract.

If it is not reasonably practicable to allow an employee returning from additional maternity leave to return to the job in which she was employed before her absence then she is entitled to a job that is suitable and appropriate for her to do. If she is to return to a different job the employee should be contacted, advised of this and given the opportunity to discuss it with her manager, the HR department, etc.

Return to Part-time Work

Requests to return on a part-time basis must be considered seriously, and a reasoned decision given if the employer does not consider part-time work to be a feasible option for the employee in question. Failure to offer part-time work if it is requested can form the basis of a claim of indirect sex discrimination and may also infringe the employee's rights in respect of the right to request flexible working.

Further Options

The following are some further options that employers might like to consider when drawing up a policy and procedures on maternity rights. The **Management of Health and Safety at Work (Amendment) Regulations 1994** introduced provisions to ensure that employers conduct a risk assessment of the work processes new, expectant and breastfeeding mothers might carry out and of any substances to which they might be exposed. Any risk to the mother or her baby which is identified must then be eliminated, or her hours of work or conditions changed so that she avoids the risk.

Furthermore, if a woman is a night worker and she produces a medical certificate which states that the night work poses a threat to her health and safety then, if possible, she should be transferred to day work. In conjunction with this legislation, provisions were introduced whereby an employee must be put on paid suspension if she cannot continue to work because a risk cannot be eliminated and no suitable alternative work can be found for her to do, or if she is a night worker and she cannot be transferred to days. The right to paid suspension came into effect under the **Suspension from Work (on Maternity Grounds) Order 1994**.

The employee has the right to work as close to her expected week of childbirth as she wishes provided she continues to be capable of doing her job and there is no risk to her health. It might also be desirable to include provision for her to be referred to an occupational doctor if the employer feels she is prejudicing her health and safety by continuing to work whilst pregnant.

Contractual Maternity Rights

Some employers grant pregnant employees more generous rights than those provided by statute. Sometimes this is done unintentionally, as where the employee is promised a part-time job on her return by her manager, which the company then has difficulty in honouring. However, some employers make a conscious decision to enhance statutory maternity rights. It is obviously just as important, if not more so, for contractual maternity schemes to be set down in writing in the form of a policy and procedure, in the same way as has been described for statutory rights. The areas in which contractual schemes tend to enhance maternity rights include:

- paying more than SMP, or making payments for a longer period
- extending maternity leave to more than 52 weeks (this includes some schemes under which women are allowed up to, say, five years as a career break to bring up a young family and still have the right to return to work at the end of this period)
- giving employees the express right to return to work on a part-time basis.

However, employers should bear in mind the following points.

- Recovery of National Insurance contributions in respect of maternity payments made is normally only possible in respect of those amounts paid by way of SMP to employees who qualify for them under the Department for Work and Pensions (DWP) rules.
- Although the European Court of Justice has held that employees are not required to receive full pay during maternity leave, maternity pay must reflect any increase in pay if it takes effect at any time from the beginning of the eight-week period used to calculate the higher rate of SMP, up to and including the end of the maternity pay period (**Statutory Maternity Pay (General) Amendment Regulations 1996** and *Gillespie and others v Northern Ireland Health and Social Services Board and others* ECJ 13 February 1996).
- Employees who have both statutory and contractual maternity rights are entitled to "composite" those rights and take the best bits of each.

- Male employees who claim that contractual maternity rights discriminate against them on grounds of their sex cannot make a successful claim. A specific exception is included in the **Sex Discrimination Act 1975** to the effect that favourable treatment of women in connection with pregnancy or childbirth is not unlawful discrimination against men.

CASE STUDIES

This fictional case study looks at some situations arising in Mr Jones' department.

Ms Brinks

Ms Brinks is on additional maternity leave and will not say when she will be returning to work, although she previously said she would not be absent for very long. At the time, the department was not fully stretched and Mr Jones had colleagues covering her work. He has now taken to calling her every Monday morning and asking her to commit herself to a date to return to work, but she will not be pinned down.

Women on additional maternity leave may return at any time within 52 weeks of the date their maternity leave started. Although Mr Jones is entitled to maintain reasonable contact with Ms Brinks whilst she is on maternity leave, this does not entitle him to pester Ms Brinks as to her return date as she has the absolute right to take her full period of 52 weeks' leave, or to elect to give eight weeks' notice of an early return date. Mr Jones has no say in the matter.

Ms Horley

Ms Horley has just given birth to her second child and has asked if she can return to work part time. Mr Jones does not want to allow this as he thinks it will set a precedent and all the women will want part-time work.

Employers needs to be careful. It is likely that refusing to allow a woman back part time when there is no objective reason why this cannot be accommodated may amount to indirect sex discrimination. Employers should also bear in mind that regulations give employees who are the parents of children under six years of age the right to request flexible working, although not an automatic right to be granted it.

Ms James

Ms James is not pregnant. She was hired recently to cover for one of the other employees on maternity leave. Mr Jones dislikes her, as does everyone else in the department. She has said "she is staying on whatever." He is now worried that he cannot get rid of her when the relevant maternity leave is over.

Employers have no cause for alarm if they tell temporary staff they have been taken on to cover maternity leave and will lose their jobs at the end of it. In this event, Ms James will probably not have been employed long enough to bring an unfair dismissal claim when she is dismissed (as one year's continuous service is required to bring a claim for unfair dismissal). However, Mr Jones must check that he told Ms James at the time that her contract would come to an end automatically on the return to work of the other employee.

Ms Taylor

Ms Taylor is over eight months' pregnant but will not give up work. She wants to work until the baby is due. Mr Jones is searching for a law which will give him an excuse to force her to give up work. She maintains that she will take off the six weeks during which she is entitled to 90% pay and no more. If she starts her maternity leave two weeks before the baby is born and then the baby is two weeks late, as could happen, she will only have two weeks at home with the baby. Can he force her to stop work when she is fit to carry on?

Not if the work is safe for the employee to do. The employer would have obligations under health and safety laws, but if the employee's work is office based it is unlikely there is any danger to her health. Women may work up to the day of the birth if they wish.

Ms Taylor has also asked for breastfeeding facilities to be made available at work and/or a room set aside for her to express breast milk when she returns. Mr Jones has refused to allow the baby in but is not sure about the other demand.

*The **Management of Health and Safety at Work (Amendment) Regulations 1994** (SI 1994 No. 2865) amended the **Management of Health and Safety at Work Regulations 1992** (SI 1992 No. 2051) and brought the EU Pregnant Workers Directive 92/85 EEC into force. There is a duty on an employer under those provisions to assess the health and safety risks to employees. This specifically includes assessing the health of women who are breastfeeding. Risks should be removed if possible and, if not, then hours of work or working conditions altered. In this case Mr Jones could simply offer Ms Taylor the use of a meeting room or an available office to accommodate her requirements.*

SAMPLE POLICIES

Antenatal Policy and Procedure

Policy
The company's policy is to grant reasonable requests for time off for antenatal care, subject to the operational needs of the business. Any employee who is pregnant and has made an appointment to receive antenatal care on the advice of a registered medical practitioner, registered midwife or registered health worker, may take time off with pay to keep the appointment. The company will comply fully with legal requirements in respect of statutory time off for antenatal care.

Procedure
Employees wishing to request time off for antenatal care must comply with the following procedure.
1. Requests for time off should be made in writing at the earliest reasonable opportunity to the employee's line manager. The expected period of absence and the purpose for which time off is required should be specified. Supporting documentary evidence of the appointment should be supplied and (except for the first appointment) a certificate stating that the employee is pregnant should be produced.
2. The line manager must consider the request in conjunction with the HR department having regard to the individual's eligibility, the relevance of the request and the needs of the business and inform the employee of management's decision.
3. In the event of an employee disputing the decision, the company's formal grievance procedure should be used.

Maternity Policy and Procedure

Policy
The company's policy is to comply with both the letter and spirit of the law on maternity rights. To this end, its aim is to inform all female employees of their entitlement to statutory maternity rights and to ensure that those rights are understood by employees who qualify.

Procedure
1. A female employee cannot be required to notify the employer of her pregnancy prior to the end of the 15th week before the expected week of childbirth (known as the "qualifying week"). An exception to this is where she is requesting time off for antenatal care, in which case sight of an appointment card can be required after the first appointment.
2. Once a manager has been notified or has become aware of an employee's pregnancy, the employee should be referred to the HR department, who will check her entitlement to statutory and contractual maternity rights and inform her of them. In particular, the employee will be informed whether she is eligible for SMP.
3. Employees must give notice in writing to start their maternity leave. This must be forwarded to _____ no later than the end of the qualifying week. Where this is not reasonably practicable, notice must be given as soon as possible with an explanation for the delay.
4. Once the employee has provided notification of her intention to take maternity leave from a specified date, she must be given written confirmation of the latest date on which she is entitled to return to work.
5. Employees must provide medical evidence of their expected week of childbirth in the form of a maternity certificate. This is available from the doctor or midwife after the 26th week of pregnancy and must be forwarded to the employer as soon as possible. No statutory maternity pay (SMP) will be payable without this certificate or an acceptable alternative.
6. The maximum entitlement to SMP is 39 weeks' payment. Employees will receive higher rate SMP in respect of the first six weeks (which is equivalent to 90% of the employee's average weekly earnings) and standard rate SMP for the remaining 33 weeks.
7. The contract of employment continues during both ordinary and additional maternity leave. During ordinary maternity leave, the employee will continue to benefit from all the terms and conditions

of employment which would have applied to her if she had not been absent, apart from remuneration. For these purposes, remuneration means sums payable to an employee by way of wages or salary. Of course, employees may receive statutory maternity pay if they satisfy the qualifying conditions.

8. During additional maternity leave the employee is entitled to the benefit of her employer's implied obligation to her of trust and confidence and any terms and conditions relating to notice of termination, redundancy compensation and disciplinary or grievance procedures. The employee remains bound by her implied obligation of good faith and any terms and conditions relating to disclosure of confidential information, notice of termination, the acceptance of gifts or other benefits, and participation in any other business.

9. The employer may, at its discretion, offer employees on maternity leave the opportunity to perform up to ten days work during maternity leave (either in a single block or as separate days). Where an employee agrees to perform some work (and there is no obligation on her to do so), this will not affect her right to receive statutory maternity pay, nor to continue her maternity leave. The type of work and the remuneration payable will be explained to the employee and may include, for example, the opportunity to attend training courses or team meetings.

   The employer will also maintain reasonable contact with employees on maternity leave, for example to discuss the employee's plans for returning to work or to provide her with an update on developments in the workplace.

10. Employees who:
    (a) are taken into legal custody, or
    (b) work for another employer during the maternity pay period must notify the company as soon as possible, as SMP must be stopped in these circumstances.

11. For employees who choose to return to work at or before the end of ordinary maternity leave, the following will apply:
    (a) The employee must give eight weeks' notice of her intended return date to _____.
    (b) The employee may not return to work during the two-week period immediately following the birth.
    (c) The employee will be entitled to return to the same job as she occupied before she began her leave.

(d) The employee's continuity of service will be preserved and the 26 weeks (or less, if the employee returns early) will count towards continuous service for all statutory and contractual purposes.

12. If an employee is unable to return to work at the end of additional maternity leave because she is ill, then the normal company rules on sickness absence will apply.

13. The employer may only postpone an employee's return from either ordinary or additional maternity leave if she fails to give eight weeks' notice of an early return date. Under these circumstances the employer is entitled to postpone her return so that the employer has the full benefit of the eight weeks' notice. However, the employer cannot use this provision to postpone the return beyond the end of her additional maternity leave. There are no other provisions for postponing an employee's return from maternity leave.

14. Managers must endeavour to ensure that, wherever possible, employees can exercise their full rights on returning to work (ie that they return to the job they left, on no less favourable terms and conditions of employment than if they had not been away).

15. Where it is not reasonably practicable to allow the employee to return to her old job after additional maternity leave, she must be offered another job which is suitable and appropriate for her to do in the circumstances. The employee must be advised of this as soon as possible and a meeting arranged with her to discuss the implications of the changed work.

16. In whatever capacity she returns to work, the employee's continuous service will be preserved and the period of her maternity leave will count for statutory purposes.

17. Any employee who is dissatisfied with any decision made in respect of her maternity rights should use the company's formal grievance procedure.

Additional clauses

A. Pregnant employees have the right not to be dismissed or subjected to any detriment for any reason related to pregnancy. Where the employee's pregnancy means that she is unable to do her job adequately, where it is unlawful for a pregnant woman to do a particular job, or where a health and safety risk to herself or her baby has been identified but cannot be eliminated, the employer may have to suspend that employee on full pay. Before such action is taken, every effort will be made to change the employee's hours of work or conditions, or to find suitable alternative work for her to do on a temporary basis.

B.   Where a pregnant employee is engaged on night work and she produces a medical certificate which states that for health and safety reasons she should not continue working at night, the employer may have to suspend that employee on full pay. Before such action is taken every effort will be made to find suitable day work for her.

C.   A pregnant employee may continue working as close to her expected week of childbirth as she wishes, provided she continues to be capable of doing her job adequately. The employer reserves the right to require the employee to be examined by an occupational doctor where it is felt that her health, or that of the baby, may suffer as a result of her continuing to work.

D.   It is a condition of employees' continued entitlement to benefits during their maternity leave that they do not work for another employer during this time without the employer's prior approval.

E.   Statutory maternity rights give employees the right to return to the same job after maternity leave. However, the company recognises that many women do not wish to return to full-time work and will attempt to accommodate the needs of employees wishing to return on a part-time basis. Employees wishing to do this should put their request in writing to _____ as soon as possible. A meeting will be arranged with _____ at which their wishes and the company's needs will be discussed and attempts made to agree a suitable arrangement.

KEY FACTS

- All pregnant employees have the right to reasonable paid time off work for antenatal appointments made on the advice of a registered medical practitioner, midwife or health visitor.
- Employers are not entitled to require an employee to rearrange her working days or hours to accommodate antenatal appointments, nor to make up for lost time by working additional hours.
- If there are risks to a pregnant employee's health and safety as a result of her working conditions or work processes, the employer must take

appropriate steps to remove her from those risks, either by altering her job duties or hours of work, transferring her to an alternative job, or suspending her on full pay.

- All pregnant employees are entitled to 52 weeks' maternity leave regardless of their length of service or the number of hours worked each week.
- The employee may not start her maternity leave before the 11th week before the expected week of childbirth (EWC) unless the baby is born before then, but apart from this restriction, the employee has the freedom to choose when to begin her maternity leave.
- If an employee is absent from work for a pregnancy-related reason after the beginning of the fourth week before her expected week of childbirth, then her maternity leave is triggered automatically.
- Statutory maternity pay (SMP) is payable to any employee continuously employed for 26 weeks by the end of the 15th week before the expected week of childbirth as long as her average weekly earnings are equal to or more than the statutory lower limit for National Insurance purposes.
- Employees are paid higher rate SMP, ie 90% of their average earnings, for the first six weeks of the maternity pay period, and the standard rate SMP, which is £108.85 per week (£112.75 from 1 April 2007), for the remaining 33 weeks.
- During ordinary maternity leave, the employee's contract of employment remains in force and the employee must continue to benefit from all her terms and conditions of employment, except remuneration, whilst more limited contractual terms remain in force during additional maternity leave.
- Employees on maternity leave may, by agreement with the employer, go into work for up to ten days (which may be either separate days or a single block) without losing their statutory maternity pay or triggering the end of maternity leave.
- If an employee decides to take the full period of maternity leave to which she is entitled, she need not give her employer any prior notice of her return date.
- If the employee wishes to return to work before the end of her 52 weeks' maternity leave, she must give her employer at least eight weeks' notice of her intended return date.
- When an employee returns to work from ordinary maternity leave, she is entitled to return to the same job she was in before she went on

leave, and on terms and conditions that are no less favourable than those which would have applied if she had not been absent.

- For an employee returning from additional maternity leave, if the employer can show that it was not reasonably practicable for her to return to the same job, the employee may be offered another job which is suitable and appropriate for her to do and which is on terms and conditions that are no less favourable than those that would have applied if she had not gone on leave.

- Requests to return to work on a part-time basis must be considered seriously with full consideration of the laws that impact on this area, and a reasoned decision given if the employer does not consider part-time work to be a feasible option.

- If a temporary replacement is recruited to replace an employee on maternity leave, the replacement will technically be engaged on a fixed-term contract terminable on the occurrence of the original employee's return to work.

- A dismissal will be automatically unfair if it is in any way due to pregnancy, childbirth or maternity leave.

- Once an employee has returned to work following ordinary or additional maternity leave, all periods of maternity leave must be counted as continuous service for the purpose of the employee's statutory rights.

CHAPTER 3

PATERNITY POLICIES, LEAVE AND ASSOCIATED ISSUES

INTRODUCTION

Paternity leave is a period of leave taken by an employee at around the time of childbirth to enable him or her to spend time with his or her family. Government research has indicated that men want to play a more active role following the arrival of a child, but that there may be a conflict between this need and the need for extra income created by the arrival of a new family member.

Paternity leave is now a legal entitlement for employees in circumstances where:

- the employee's wife or partner gives birth to a child
- the employee adopts a child jointly with his/her spouse or civil partner, provided the employee has not elected to take adoption leave
- the employee's partner adopts a child, provided the employee has not chosen to take adoption leave.

Paternity leave is available only to employees (and not other workers or self-employed people) and is unaffected if more than one child is born or placed for adoption as part of the same pregnancy or placement.

LEGAL REQUIREMENTS — A SUMMARY

An eligible employee will have the right:

- to take one or two weeks' paternity leave and resume normal working afterwards
- to receive statutory paternity pay

- not to be subjected to a detriment or dismissed for a reason related to the fact that the he or she has requested or taken a period of paternity leave.

PATERNITY LEAVE

Since 6 April 2003, employees who are eligible are entitled to take paid paternity leave in order to care for their new baby and/or support the mother of the child.

Qualifying Conditions for Paternity Leave

An employee may be eligible to take paternity leave in respect of either a birth child or an adopted child provided he or she is:
- the biological father of the child
- married to, or the partner of, the child's mother (and not the biological father of the child)
- the same-sex partner of the child's mother (thus entitling women in certain circumstances to paternity leave)
- married to or the partner of someone who is adopting a child under age 18 (irrespective of whether the employee is male or female)
- the same-sex partner of the child's adopter (whether male or female).

In all cases, the employee must live with the child's mother or adopter in an enduring family relationship and have, or expect to have, responsibility for the child's upbringing.

To qualify for the right to take paternity leave, the employee must also have a minimum of 26 weeks' continuous service as at the end of the "qualifying week" (in the case of a birth child) or the end of the "relevant week" (in the case of an adopted child).

The "qualifying week" is the 15th week before the employee's partner's baby is due to be born.

The "relevant week" is the week in which the child's adopter receives formal notification from the adoption agency that he or she has been matched with a child.

Where an employee's child is stillborn, he or she will only be entitled to take statutory paternity leave if the stillbirth occurs after the 24th week of pregnancy.

Another criterion for eligibility for paternity leave is that the employee must have earnings that are equal to or higher than the lower earnings limit for National Insurance purposes (£84 per week — £87 per week from 1 April 2007).

Notification Requirements

In order to take statutory paternity leave after the birth of a child, an employee must have:

- formally notified the employer of his or her intention to take statutory paternity leave
- provided documentary evidence supporting his or her right to take statutory paternity leave, if requested.

Notification must be provided by the end of the qualifying week for a birth child or within seven days of the end of the relevant week in respect of an adopted child, and must state how much leave the employee wishes to take (one or two weeks) and the date on which leave is to begin. The week in which the child is expected to be born or placed for adoption should also be stated.

Notification does not need to be given in writing. However, if the employer requests it, the employee must provide a signed declaration that he or she satisfies the conditions of entitlement to statutory paternity leave and that his or her absence from work will be for the purpose of caring for the child or supporting the child's mother or adopter.

If, having provided notification of his or her intention to take statutory paternity leave on a specified date, the employee wishes to change the start date, he or she must give the employer at least 28 days' notice as to the revised start date (whether this is earlier or later than the start date originally notified). Notice of the variation should be given as soon as possible, and must be in writing if the employer requests it.

In all cases, once the baby has been born or the child has been placed for adoption, the employee must inform the employer of the date of birth or placement. Again, this must be in writing, if the employer requests it.

Timing and Duration of Statutory Paternity Leave

Statutory paternity leave is for a maximum of two weeks and employees can choose to take either one week's leave or two consecutive weeks. The legislation does not permit an employee to take paternity leave as two separate weeks or over a number of non-consecutive days.

Paternity leave may begin on any day of the week, which may include the day on which the child is born or adopted. Leave must, however, be taken within eight weeks of the birth of the child or, in the case of adoption, within eight weeks of the child's placement.

If the employee's baby is born late, the employee must delay the start of the leave until the baby is actually born.

It is not permitted for a prospective father to take statutory paternity leave before the birth of a baby, for example to accompany his partner to antenatal appointments.

Terms and Conditions during Statutory Paternity Leave

During statutory paternity leave, an employee's contract of employment continues in force and, apart from remuneration, he or she is entitled to the continuation of all terms and conditions of employment.

This means that the employee should be treated as if he or she were not absent from work and all benefits and perks should continue. In the same way, the employee is bound by any obligations that arise under the contract of employment, for example the duty of good faith and the duty of confidentiality.

The Right to Return to Work

Employees returning to work after one or two weeks' statutory paternity leave have the right to return to the job that they held immediately before their leave began, on the same terms and conditions of employment.

There is no requirement for an employee who is on paternity leave to give the employer any notice of his or her return date.

Protection from Detriment and Dismissal

If an employee is subjected to any unfavourable treatment at work for a reason related to the fact he or she has applied for or taken paternity leave, he or she may complain to an employment tribunal. The law protects employees from detrimental treatment on such grounds.

Similarly, if an employee is dismissed for any reason connected with paternity leave, the dismissal will be automatically unfair. No qualifying service is needed to claim unfair dismissal in such circumstances.

STATUTORY PATERNITY PAY

An employee who fulfils the eligibility criteria for statutory paternity leave will also be entitled to statutory paternity pay (SPP), provided he or she:

- is still employed as at the date the child is born or placed for adoption

- has earnings that are at least equal to or greater than the lower earnings limit for national insurance contributions, currently £84 per week (£87 per week from 1 April 2007).

As is the case for eligibility for statutory maternity pay and statutory adoption pay, "normal weekly earnings" are calculated by averaging the employee's actual weekly earnings (including overtime, bonus, etc) during the period of eight weeks up to and including the qualifying week or the relevant week, as appropriate.

Statutory paternity pay is a flat weekly rate, currently £108.85 per week (£112.75 per week from 1 April 2007), which is the same as the standard flat rate in force for statutory maternity pay and statutory adoption pay. However, if 90% of the employee's normal weekly earnings amounts to less than this, then the employee's entitlement will instead be to receive a sum equivalent to that figure, ie to be paid 90% of his or her normal weekly earnings.

Recovery of Statutory Paternity Pay

All employers can recover statutory paternity pay paid to employees. Most employers can recover 92% of the sums paid. Small employers can recover 100% of statutory paternity pay, plus 4.5% National Insurance compensation.

To be classified as a small employer, the gross National Insurance contributions of the business (employees and employers) in the last qualifying tax year must be less than £45,000.

FUTURE DEVELOPMENTS

The Government has published a proposal to increase the rate of statutory paternity pay from its current level (which is a flat weekly rate) to a sum equivalent to 90% of the employee's actual average earnings. This would be in line with the higher rate of statutory maternity pay, payable to women during the first six weeks of their maternity leave.

There is a separate proposal to introduce a new statutory right to 26 weeks additional paternity leave and additional paternity pay for fathers/partners during the second six months of their wife's/partner's maternity or adoption leave, provided the latter is employed and has returned to work. This will be in addition to the two weeks paternity leave available to fathers/partners during the first eight weeks following the birth or adoption of the child.

Fathers will, if eligible, be able to take additional paternity leave once the child is at least 20 weeks old. Additional paternity leave will have to be taken in a single block and be complete by the child's first birthday. If the mother, at the time of her return to work, has some of her entitlement to SMP or SAP left, the father will be entitled to be paid an equivalent amount of SPP (statutory paternity pay) whilst on leave.

SAMPLE POLICY

Paternity Policy and Procedure

Policy
The Company encourages employees to have a balance between their work and family commitments, believing that this ensures a more effective and efficient workforce.

This policy has been developed to provide you with guidance as to your entitlements and the procedure to follow if requesting paternity leave.

No employee will be treated less favourably, suffer detriment or be dismissed because he or she requests or takes paternity leave. However, the misuse of paternity leave, such as the use of leave for reasons other than to care for the child or support the mother, or failure to follow the correct procedure, may result in disciplinary action being taken against you.

Procedure
1. Paternity leave is the right to take paid leave to care for a child or support the mother.
2. In order to qualify for paternity leave in birth situations you must:
    (a) be the child's biological father, and have, or expect to have, the main responsibility for the child's upbringing
    (b) be the spouse or partner of the mother, and have, or expect to have, the main responsibility for the child's upbringing.
3. In order to qualify for paternity leave in adoptive situations you must be married to, or the partner of, the adopter, and have, or expect to have, the main responsibility for the child's upbringing.
4. In both birth and adoptive situations you must:
    (a) have formally notified your manager of your intention to take statutory paternity leave
    (b) have provided documentary evidence (Inland Revenue form SC3 or SC4) supporting your right to take statutory paternity leave, if requested by your manager.

5. Paternity leave is for a maximum of two weeks. You may take the leave in a block of one or two consecutive weeks. Leave must be taken within 56 days of the birth of the child or, in the case of adoption, within eight weeks of the placement.

6. In order to take statutory paternity leave after the birth of a child, you must inform your manager of your intention to take leave by the end of the 15th week before the mother's expected week of childbirth (EWC). You must specify:
   (a) the week in which the baby is expected to be born
   (b) whether you intend to take one or two weeks' leave
   (c) the date on which you intend to start your leave.

7. In order to take statutory paternity leave after the adoption of a child, you must notify your manager of your intention to take leave no later than seven days after the date on which you or your partner received notification from the adoption agency of the match with the child. If the child was adopted from abroad you must let your employer know the date on which you received notification of the placement and the date on which the child is expected to enter the UK.

8. Statutory paternity leave may not be taken before the birth or adoption of a child.

9. If you fall ill before starting your period of paternity leave, you should postpone it. The 56-day period within which you should take your leave is not extended under these circumstances.

10. You may be entitled to statutory paternity pay (SPP). Your manager will let you know whether you are. SPP is currently paid at the rate of £108.85 per week (£112.75 per week from 1 April 2007). Should you not qualify for SPP you may be able to get income support while on paternity leave. Your local social security office will be able to advise.

11. You are entitled to return to the same job as before, on the same terms and conditions of employment, unless a redundancy situation arises. It is presumed that you will return to work after a period of paternity leave.

12. If you cannot return to work at the end of your paternity leave because of illness, you should follow the normal procedures for sickness absence.

13. If you do not wish to return to work, you are required to give your manager notice in accordance with your contractual notice period.

KEY FACTS

- An employee whose wife or partner gives birth to a child, or who adopts a child, may be eligible for statutory paternity leave.
- To qualify for the right to take paternity leave, the employee must have a minimum of 26 weeks' continuous service as at the end of the "qualifying week" (in the case of a birth child) or the end of the "relevant week" (in the case of an adopted child).
- Statutory paternity leave is for a maximum of two weeks and employees can choose to take either one week's leave or two consecutive weeks. The legislation does not permit an employee to take paternity leave as two separate weeks or over a number of non-consecutive days.
- Statutory paternity leave must be taken within eight weeks of the birth of the child or, in the case of adoption, within eight weeks of the child's placement.
- During paternity leave, an employee's contract of employment continues in force and, apart from remuneration, the employee is entitled to the continuation of all terms and conditions of employment.
- An employee is entitled not to be subjected to any detriment, or dismissed, on account of applying for or taking paternity leave.
- An employee who fulfils the eligibility criteria for statutory paternity leave will also be entitled to statutory paternity pay, provided he or she is still employed as at the date the child is born or placed for adoption and has earnings that are at least equal to or greater than the lower earnings limit for National Insurance contributions.

CHAPTER 4

ADOPTION POLICIES, LEAVE AND ASSOCIATED ISSUES

INTRODUCTION

In April 2003, a new statutory right was introduced for employees to take time off work to care for a child who had been newly placed with them for adoption. The period of available leave is up to 52 weeks, and the rules and procedures applicable to statutory adoption leave and statutory adoption pay are the same in many respects as those applicable to statutory maternity leave and pay.

The right to adoption leave and pay exists in relation to the adoption of a child of any age up to age 18 from an approved adoption agency. An employee may also qualify for adoption leave in respect of an overseas adoption.

Adoption leave is available only to employees (and not other workers or self-employed people) and is unaffected if more than one child is placed for adoption as part of the same placement.

Where a couple adopts a child jointly, only one of them may take statutory adoption leave.

LEGAL REQUIREMENTS — A SUMMARY

An eligible employee who is individually or jointly (as part of a couple) adopting a child may take up to 26 weeks' ordinary adoption leave, immediately followed by up to 26 weeks' additional adoption leave.

Employees whose average weekly earnings are equal to or above the lower earnings limit (currently £84 — £87 from 1 April 2007) are also entitled to be paid up to 26 weeks' statutory adoption pay during their ordinary adoption leave period.

ADOPTION LEAVE

Employees who meet the criteria for eligibility are entitled to take paid adoption leave in order to look after and form a relationship with the adopted child. Men and women are both eligible.

Where a couple adopts a child jointly, only one of them may take statutory adoption leave (the couple can choose which). The other partner may, if eligible, take statutory paternity leave.

Qualifying Conditions for Adoption Leave

An employee may be eligible to take adoption leave in respect of an adopted child under age 18 (whether adopted in the UK or from overseas), provided he or she is:

- the adopter of the child
- married to or the partner of someone who is adopting a child (irrespective of whether the employee is male or female)
- the same-sex partner of the child's adopter (whether male or female).

Adoption leave is not, however, available to step-parents who adopt their partner's child, nor to foster parents who have previously fostered the child they adopt. This is because adoption leave is available only to those with whom an adopted child is *newly placed*.

To qualify for adoption leave, the employee must have:

- been continuously employed for at least 26 weeks by the end of the week in which he or she (or his or her spouse or partner) was formally notified by an approved adoption agency of being matched with a child for adoption — this is known as the "relevant week"
- notified the agency that he or she agrees with the placement
- complied with the notification requirements
- (in the case of an employee whose partner is adopting a child) expect to have joint responsibility for the child's upbringing.

Notification Requirements

Adoption within the UK
To exercise the right to adoption leave, eligible employees must do the following:

- inform their employers of their intention to take statutory adoption leave within seven days of having been notified by the adoption agency that they and/or their partner have been matched with a child for adoption
- provide documentary evidence in the form of a certificate provided by the adoption agency if requested by the employer
- advise their employer of the date on which the child is expected to be placed with them for adoption and when they want their adoption leave to start.

Adoption from overseas
Eligible employees adopting a child from overseas must do the following:

- inform their employers of their intention to take adoption leave within 28 days of receiving an official notification from the relevant domestic authority
- notify their employers of the date on which the official notification was received
- produce a copy of that notification if asked to do so by the employer
- inform their employers of the date the child is expected to enter Britain.

Once the child enters Britain, the employee must give the employer at least 28 days' advance notice of the date on which adoption leave is to start, as well as evidence (eg a plane ticket receipt) confirming the child's arrival.

Notification of Change of Start Date

An employee is entitled to change the date when he or she intends to start statutory adoption leave, providing:

- he or she gives the employer at least 28 days' notice of the new date, whether it falls earlier or later than the original notified date
- puts the request in writing, if the employer requests it.

If it is not reasonably practicable for the employee to give 28 days' notice of the change, then he or she must notify the employer as soon as possible.

Responding to an Employee's Notification

Once the employer has been notified of the date on which an eligible employee intends to start his or her adoption leave, it must write to the employee within 28 days setting out the date the employee would be expected to return to work if his or her full entitlement to adoption leave is taken.

An employer who does not write to the employee within the 28-day period loses the right to prevent the employee returning to work before the end of his or her statutory adoption leave without giving notice, or to dismiss or discipline the employee for returning to work after the due return date.

Timing and Duration of Statutory Adoption Leave

Adoption leave consists of two parts:
- ordinary adoption leave — which lasts for 26 weeks
- additional adoption leave — which begins the day after ordinary adoption leave ends and lasts for a further 26 weeks.

The eligibility criteria are the same for both; however, the status of the contract of employment (see below) is different for each of the two periods.

In the case of a child adopted within the UK, the employee can choose to start the adoption leave from the date of the child's placement or from a fixed date, which can be up to 14 days before the expected date of placement.

Where a child is adopted from overseas, the period of adoption may begin on the date the child enters Britain or on a pre-determined date that is no later than 28 days after the child entered Britain.

Adoption leave may be taken only in a single block and not in instalments. If the employee decides to return to work before the expiry of the total period of adoption leave, he or she will lose any outstanding entitlement.

STATUTORY ADOPTION PAY

Statutory adoption pay (SAP) is payable to eligible employees for the first 39 weeks of adoption leave at a flat weekly rate. The rate is currently £108.85 per week — £112.75 from 1 April 2007 (the same as the standard flat rate in force for statutory maternity pay (SMP) and statutory paternity pay (SPP)). However, if 90% of the employee's normal weekly earnings amounts to less than this, then the employee's entitlement will instead be to receive a sum equivalent to that figure, ie to be paid 90% of his or her normal weekly earnings. Entitlement to statutory adoption pay is not dependent on the employee's decision whether or not to return to work after adoption leave.

Statutory adoption pay must be stopped if the employee returns to work early, or begins work for another employer, irrespective of whether the employee's total entitlement has been used up at that point.

In order to be eligible to receive statutory adoption pay, the employee must have normal weekly earnings that are at least equivalent to the lower earnings limit for national insurance purposes, which is currently £84 per week (£87 from 1 April 2007). "Normal weekly earnings" are calculated by averaging the employee's actual weekly earnings (including overtime, bonus, etc) during the period of eight weeks up to and including the "relevant week" (ie the week during which the adopter was given formal notification of the match with the child).

If an eligible employee resigns or is dismissed after the relevant week, but before the start of adoption leave, he or she will retain entitlement to receive statutory adoption pay. In this case, payment must begin 14 days before the expected date of the child's placement.

The remaining 13 weeks of additional adoption leave is unpaid, unless the employer chooses to continue full or part salary during all or part of adoption leave.

The government has stated an intention to extend statutory adoption pay to 52 weeks by the end of the current parliament. When this occurs, employees who qualify will be entitled to receive SAP throughout the whole of their period of adoption leave.

Recovery of Statutory Adoption Pay

All employers can recover statutory adoption pay paid to employees. Most employers can recover 92% of the sums paid. Small employers can recover 100% of statutory adoption pay, plus 4.5% National Insurance compensation.

To be classified as a small employer, the gross National Insurance contributions of the business (employees and employers) in the last qualifying tax year must be less than £45,000.

The rules in respect of keeping records are the same as for statutory maternity pay.

EMPLOYEES' RIGHTS DURING ADOPTION LEAVE

A employee's contract of employment continues throughout both ordinary and additional adoption leave.

Rights and Duties during Ordinary Adoption Leave

During ordinary adoption leave, the employee must continue to benefit from all normal terms and conditions of employment, except remuneration (statutory adoption pay will be payable instead). Some organisations may choose to continue full or part salary/wages through all or part of the employee's adoption leave.

Rights and Duties during Additional Adoption Leave

During additional adoption leave, the situation is different. The law requires that the terms relating to notice of termination, redundancy pay and disciplinary and grievance procedures must apply. The position as regards an employee's entitlement to accrue statutory annual holiday during additional adoption leave is, at present, not clear. To be safe, employers should assume that statutory annual holiday will continue to accrue during additional adoption leave, as well as during ordinary adoption leave. Furthermore, mutual trust and confidence continues to apply. All other terms and conditions of employment may, however, be suspended during additional adoption leave. Nevertheless, the employer should make it clear through its policies and procedures if it intends to stop contractual benefits during additional adoption leave.

An employee on additional adoption leave remains bound by the implied obligation of good faith to the employer and any terms relating to notice, disclosure of confidential information, acceptance of gifts or other benefits and participation in any other business.

Disrupted Placement

If after an employee has begun adoption leave:
- the expected placement does not occur
- the newly-adopted child dies
- the child is returned to the adoption agency

the employee's adoption leave period ends eight weeks after the start of the ordinary adoption leave period (if the placement did not occur), or eight weeks from the end of the week in which death occurred or the child was returned to the agency (if the placement did take place and the disruption occurred later).

Keeping in Touch Days

A new provision permitting "keeping in touch days" was introduced in respect of employees whose child was expected to be placed for adoption on or after 1 April 2007. This provision allows an employee on adoption leave to go into work for up to ten days (which may be either separate days or a single block) without losing his or her statutory adoption pay in respect of those days or triggering the end of the adoption leave period. For this provision to operate, both the employer and the employee must agree:

• that the employee will do some work
• the type of work, for example attendance at a training course
• the amount of remuneration that will be payable in respect of the work done (the employer can offset the SAP paid in respect of the working days against wages/salary).

This provision does not allow an employer to insist that an employee on adoption leave should come in to work, nor does it confer a right on the employee to be offered any work.

Reasonable Contact

Over and above the "keeping in touch days" discussed above, employers may maintain reasonable contact with employees on adoption leave. This may, for example, be in order to discuss the employee's plans for returning to work or to provide an update on developments in the workplace.

RIGHT TO RETURN TO WORK

If an employee decides to take the full period of adoption leave to which he or she is entitled, there is no need to give the employer any prior notice of the return date. The employee may simply return on the first working day after full entitlement to adoption leave has ended, in accordance with the date notified by the employer.

As is the case for maternity leave, there is no requirement for employees to use the whole period of adoption leave available to them.

Early Return

If employees wishes to return to work before the end of the statutory adoption leave period, they must give the employer at least eight weeks' notice of the intended return date. If they attempt to come back to work without having done this, then the employer may postpone their return to a date that will provide eight weeks' notice. The employer may not, however, use this provision to postpone their return beyond the date when their adoption leave was due to end anyway.

If an employer has not given employees proper notice of when they were due to return to work in the first place, they cannot be prevented from coming back early, even if they have not given the correct notice.

Apart from the provisions noted above, there are no other circumstances in which it is lawful for either the employer or the employee to postpone the employee's return to work beyond the end of statutory adoption leave.

Sickness at the End of Adoption Leave

If employees cannot return to work at the end of adoption leave because of illness, they should notify the employer in accordance with the normal company rules relating to sickness absence. If they qualify, they should be paid SSP and/or company sick pay in the normal way. In effect, the day on which an employee should have returned will be the first day in a period of sickness absence.

Resignation

If employees decide not to return from adoption leave at all, they must give the employer notice of resignation in accordance with the terms of their contract. Employment will then come to an end at the end of their notice period. This will not affect entitlement to SAP.

Rights on Return from Ordinary Adoption Leave

When employees return to work at or before the end of ordinary adoption leave, they are entitled to return to the same job they were in before the start of adoption leave, on terms and conditions that are no less favourable than those that would have applied if the absence had not taken place. Seniority and other similar rights must also be the same as they would have been if the employees had not been absent.

"Job" in this context means the nature of the work which the employee is employed to do in accordance with the contract and the capacity and place in which the employee is employed.

Rights on Return from Additional Adoption Leave

When employees return from additional adoption leave, they are entitled to return to their old job unless the employer can show that it was not reasonably practicable for this to happen. In these circumstances, the employee must be offered another job that is suitable and appropriate, and that is on terms and conditions that are no less favourable than those that would have applied if the employee had not gone on adoption leave. Where employment rights depend on seniority, the employee's employment before going on leave should be treated as continuous with his or her employment after coming back to work.

If there has been a general pay rise during the employee's adoption leave, wages/salary should be increased accordingly on the employee's return.

PROTECTION FROM DETRIMENT AND DISMISSAL

If an employee is subjected to any unfavourable treatment at work for a reason related to the fact that he or she took adoption leave, he or she may complain to an employment tribunal. The law protects employees from detrimental treatment on such grounds.

Similarly, if an employee is dismissed for any reason connected with the fact he or she applied for or took adoption leave, the dismissal will be automatically unfair. No qualifying service is needed to claim unfair dismissal in such circumstances.

SAMPLE POLICIES

Adoption Policy and Procedure

Policy
The Organisation encourages employees to have a balance between their work and family commitments, believing that it ensures a more effective and efficient workforce.

This Adoption Leave Policy has been developed to provide you with guidance as to your entitlements and the procedure to follow for adoption leave. Adoption leave is the right to take paid leave when a child up to 18 years of age is newly placed with you for adoption.

No employee will be treated less favourably, suffer detriment, or be dismissed because he or she requests, or takes, adoption leave. However, the misuse of adoption leave such as the use of leave for reasons other than to care for the child or support the mother, or failure to follow the correct procedure may result in disciplinary action being taken against you.

Procedure
1. To qualify for adoption leave you will need to satisfy the following conditions. You must:
   (a) be newly matched* with a child for adoption by an approved adoption agency
   (b) have worked continuously for the organisation for 26 weeks leading into the week in which you are notified of being matched with a child for adoption
   (c) forward your Matching Certificate from your adoption agency to the HR department 28 days before you wish your adoption leave to commence. This is evidence of adoption to qualify for your entitlement to adoption leave and pay.
   Where parents adopt jointly, it will be for them to choose who should take adoption leave.
   Adoption leave and pay will not apply where a child is not newly matched for adoption, eg when a step-parent is adopting a partner's child or adoptions by foster carers where there is already an established relationship.
2. Adoption leave and pay is available to:
   (a) individuals who adopt
   (b) one member of a couple where a couple adopts jointly (the couple may choose which partner takes adoption leave).
3. Those who are eligible are entitled to up to a total of 52 weeks' leave as follows:
   (a) 26 weeks' ordinary adoption leave
   (b) 26 weeks' additional adoption leave.
   You can choose to start your leave:
   (a) on the date of the child's placement
   (b) on a fixed date, which can be up to 14 days before the expected date of placement
   (c) on any day of the week.
   You are only entitled to one period of leave even if more than one child is placed for adoption.

You must notify the HR department that you intend to take adoption leave within seven days of being notified by your adoption agency that they have matched you with a child for adoption, or as soon as reasonably practicable.

You must tell us when:

(a) the child is expected to be placed with you

(b) when you want your adoption leave to start.

Should you wish to change the date on which you want your leave to start, you must give us at least 28 days' notice of the new start date.

If you intend to return to work before the end of your adoption leave period, you must write to the HR department giving eight weeks' notice of your date of return.

4. If you are eligible for adoption leave, you will also be eligible to receive statutory adoption pay (SAP) for the first 39 weeks of your adoption leave, provided you earn more than £84 per week on average (£87 from 1 April 2007). SAP is paid at a flat rate of £108.85 per week (£112.75 per week from 1 April 2007) or 90% of your average weekly earnings if these are less than this. The remaining 13 weeks of adoption leave are unpaid. Should you not qualify for SAP you may be able to seek financial support from your Local Authority. Additional financial support may be available through:

(a) housing benefit

(b) council tax benefit

(c) tax credits.

5. Your contractual rights and benefits remain in place while you are on 52 weeks' adoption leave except for the terms relating to your salary (unless the organisation using this as a template has a contract of employment that states otherwise).

6. It is presumed that you will return to work at the end of your full adoption leave entitlement. However, if you intend to return to work before the end of your adoption leave period you must write to the HR department giving at least eight weeks' notice of your intended date of return. If you fail to do so, the organisation may delay your return until the eight week period has expired, or the end of your adoption leave period, whichever is earlier.

7. You are entitled to return to the same job as before on the same terms and conditions of employment at the end of ordinary adoption leave, unless a redundancy situation has arisen.

8. You are entitled to return to the same job at the end of your additional adoption leave, unless it is not practicable for you to do so. In such

circumstances you will be offered any available comparable position for your skills and experience, on no less favourable terms and conditions.

If you cannot return to work at the end of your full adoption leave period because of illness, you should follow the normal contractual procedures for sickness absence as laid out in the terms and conditions of employment.

If you do not wish to return to work, you are required to give the organisation notice in accordance with your contractual notice period, as set out in your term and conditions of employment.

9. Procedure for Adoption Leave is as follows.

Employee to:

(a) inform the HR department you are adopting, within seven days of being notified, and confirm when the child is expected to be placed with you and when you want your adoption leave to commence

(b) forward Matching Certificate as proof.

HR department to:

(a) send employee confirmation letter detailing adoption leave pay and leave entitlements

(b) inform payroll and pension administrator.

Employee to:

(a) give eight weeks' notice, if intend to return before end of full adoption leave entitlement

(b) give notice under the contract of employment if intend not to return to work.

KEY FACTS

- An eligible employee who is individually or jointly (as part of a couple) adopting a child may take up to 26 weeks' ordinary adoption leave immediately followed by up to 26 weeks' additional adoption leave.
- Where a couple adopts a child jointly, only one of them may take statutory adoption leave although the other partner may, if eligible, take statutory paternity leave.
- To qualify for the right to take adoption leave, the employee must have a minimum of 26 weeks' continuous service as at the end of the "relevant week", which is the week in which formal notification of the child's placement is received from an approved adoption agency.

- The eligibility criteria are the same for both ordinary adoption leave and additional adoption leave; however the status of the contract of employment is different for each of the two periods.
- In the case of a child adopted within the UK, the employee can choose to start his or her adoption leave from the date of the child's placement or from a fixed date, which can be up to 14 days before the expected date of placement.
- An employee who fulfils the eligibility criteria for statutory adoption leave will also be entitled to statutory adoption pay, provided he or she is still employed in the "relevant week" and has earnings that are at least equal to or greater than the lower earnings limit for National Insurance contributions.
- Entitlement to statutory adoption pay is not dependent on the employee's decision whether or not to return to work after adoption leave.
- During ordinary adoption leave, the employee's contract of employment remains in force and the employee must continue to benefit from all his or her terms and conditions of employment, except remuneration, whilst more limited contractual terms remain in force during additional adoption leave.
- Employees on adoption leave may, by agreement with the employer, go into work for up to ten days (which may be either separate days or a single block) without losing their statutory adoption pay or triggering the end of adoption leave.
- An employee who decides to take the full period of adoption leave to which he or she is entitled need not give the employer any prior notice of his or her return date, but if the employee wishes to return early, he or she must give the employer at least eight weeks' notice.
- If an employee returns to work by the end of ordinary adoption leave, he or she is entitled to return to the same job. However, for an employee returning from additional adoption leave, the employer may, if it can show that it was not reasonably practicable for the employee to return to the same job, offer the employee another job that is suitable and appropriate and which is on terms and conditions that are no less favourable than those that would have applied if the employee had not taken adoption leave.
- An employee is entitled not to be subjected to any detriment, or be dismissed, on account of applying for or taking adoption leave.

CHAPTER 5

PARENTAL LEAVE

INTRODUCTION

The **Maternity and Parental Leave Regulations 1999** created a right for employees — both men and women — to take parental leave and came into effect on 15 December 1999. This right to parental leave operates independently of the rights to maternity leave and paternity leave and applies to both natural and adoptive parents and anyone who has acquired formal parental responsibility for a child. Part-time employees have the same entitlement (on a pro-rata basis) as full-time employees. Only employees qualify, ie other workers such as sub-contractors, freelance workers and casual workers have no entitlement to parental leave.

LEGAL REQUIREMENTS — A SUMMARY

Where an employee qualifies for parental leave, he or she is entitled to take a total of 13 weeks' leave (although not necessarily all at once). This entitlement arises for each child and for both parents. There is a one-year qualifying period of service. All periods of parental leave are unpaid unless the employer chooses to pay the employee full or part wage/salary during the leave.

PARENTAL LEAVE ENTITLEMENTS

Who Qualifies?

To qualify for parental leave, an employee must have at least one year's continuous service with his or her employer as at the date parental leave is to start, and must:

- be the parent (named on the birth certificate) of a child who is under the age of five, or a disabled child under the age of 18, or
- have acquired formal parental responsibility under the **Children Act 1989** (or its Scottish equivalent) for a child who is under five years old, or a disabled child under the age of 18, or
- have adopted a child under the age of 18.

The only other eligibility requirement is that the employee must have, or expect to have, responsibility for the child in question and be taking the leave for the purpose of caring for the child. There is, however, no requirement for the employee to live with the child full time (as is the case for entitlement to take paternity leave). Thus, for example, a divorced or separated father may legitimately request a period of parental leave provided the purpose of the leave is to spend time with his child.

Timing and Duration of Parental Leave

An employee who qualifies for parental leave is entitled to take a total of 13 weeks' leave in respect of each individual child. Thus, where an employee has more than one child, he or she is entitled to 13 weeks in respect of each one. Similarly, in the case of twins, triplets, etc, the employee is entitled to 13 weeks' parental leave for each child.

Where the child in respect of whom parental leave is taken is disabled, the amount of parental leave available to each parent is 18 weeks.

In most cases, parental leave may only be taken up until the child's fifth birthday. An exception is made for the parents of a disabled child (ie where the child is entitled to a disability living allowance), who may take parental leave up until the child's 18th birthday. Parents of an adopted child may take leave up until the fifth anniversary of the date on which the child was placed with them for adoption (or the child's 18th birthday if that occurs sooner).

In cases where the employee would have taken parental leave on or before these end dates but for the fact that the employer postponed it under the Government's fallback scheme (see below), then the dates are extended.

The total amount of parental leave available to an eligible employee is unaffected if an employee changes jobs. Thus, for example, if an employee has taken six weeks' parental leave with a previous employer, this must be taken into account and, after one year's service with a new employer, the employee will have the right to take up to a further seven weeks' parental leave (provided the child is still under five years of age at the relevant time, or under age 18 if adopted or disabled).

Meaning of a Week's Leave

Unless agreed otherwise through a relevant agreement, employees may not take parental leave in less than blocks of one week. An exception to this principle is made in relation to the parents of a disabled child, who may take parental leave in blocks of less than a week and even in single days. In this case, the amounts of parental leave taken may be added together to determine when a week's leave has been taken.

Where the period for which an employee is normally required to work in the course of a week does not vary, then a week's parental leave is a period of absence equal to the period he or she is normally required to work.

Where the period the employee is normally required to work varies, then a week's parental leave is a period of absence calculated by dividing the total of the periods he or she is normally required to work in a year by 52.

Notice of Parental Leave

An employee who wishes to take a period of parental leave must give his or her employer at least 21 days' notice, stating the dates on which the period of parental leave is to begin and end. Notice need not be in writing. This period of notice may be varied through an agreement with the workforce, either upwards or downwards.

If requested by the employer, the employee must:

- produce evidence that he or she has formal parental responsibility for the child in respect of whom parental leave is requested
- state the child's date of birth, and, in the case of an adopted child, the date on which the child was placed for adoption

- in the case of a disabled child, produce evidence of entitlement to disability living allowance.

Rights and Obligations during Parental Leave

Employees remain employed during periods of parental leave although most contractual terms, including pay, may be suspended unless the employee is entitled to continue to receive defined benefits under the terms of his or her contract. Employers must, however, continue to honour any terms and conditions relating to notice of termination, redundancy compensation and disciplinary and grievance procedures. The position as regards an employee's entitlement to accrue statutory annual holiday during parental leave is not clear. To be safe, employers should assume that statutory annual holiday continues to accrue during all periods of parental leave. Employers remain bound by their implied obligation of trust and confidence.

Employees, for their part, remain bound by their implied obligation of good faith, and any terms and conditions relating to disclosure of confidential information, notice of termination, the acceptance of gifts or other benefits, and their participation in any other business.

Right to Return to Work after Parental Leave

Employees who take parental leave for a period of four weeks or less are entitled to return to their old jobs. An employee who takes parental leave for a period of more than four weeks is entitled either to return to their old job or, if that is not reasonably practicable, to another job which is suitable and appropriate for them to do.

Employees must be permitted to return from parental leave on terms and conditions that are not less favourable than those that would have applied if they had not been absent. If there has been a general pay increase during the employee's parental leave, the employee will be entitled to be granted the rise on return to work. Similarly, seniority, pension rights and other rights dependent on length of service must be no less favourable than they would have been if the employee had worked normally instead of taking parental leave.

Once an employee has returned from parental leave, the period of leave must be counted as continuous service.

PARENTAL LEAVE SCHEMES

Employers and employees are free to agree their own parental leave schemes through collective, workforce or individual agreements, provided these contain certain key elements prescribed by statute and are incorporated into employees' contracts of employment. Where employers and employees do not reach their own agreements about parental leave, then the Government's fallback scheme automatically comes into operation (see below). Employers and employees may, of course, adopt the fallback scheme by choice.

Agreements

An employer may, through discussions with employees or their representatives, set up a collective agreement, workforce agreement or individual agreements in order to regulate the detail of how parental leave will work for its employees. Such agreements may not reduce the key statutory rights set out in the Regulations, but may modify such matters as notice, postponement and how much parental leave can be taken at once.

Collective agreement

A collective agreement is an agreement made between one or more independent trade unions and one or more employers or employers' associations.

Workforce agreement

This is an agreement reached between an employer and its employees or their representatives where they are not covered by a collective agreement. To be valid, the agreement must:

- be in writing
- have effect for a specified period of not more than five years, and
- be signed by elected representatives of either the entire workforce or the particular group to whom it applies; where, however, an employer has 20 or fewer employees, either elected representatives or a majority of the employees must sign the agreement.

All those affected by the agreement must be supplied with a copy of it before it is signed, together with any guidance needed in order for them to understand it.

PARENTAL LEAVE

Individual agreement

The employer may elect to reach agreement about how parental leave will work with each employee individually, for example by including terms about parental leave in each employee's contract of employment.

The Fallback Scheme

The Government's fallback scheme applies to employees who are not subject to a collective agreement, workforce agreement or individual agreement covering parental leave. The fallback scheme contains the following provisions.

Employees may not take parental leave unless:

- they have given the employer proper notice of the period of leave they intend to take, and
- they have complied with any request by the employer to produce evidence relating to their responsibility for the child in question, the child's date of birth (or date of adoption) and, where relevant, entitlement to disability living allowance.

An employee may not go ahead and take parental leave if the employer has postponed it (see below).

Minimum period of leave

Under the fallback scheme, employees may only take parental leave in blocks or multiples of one week. This rule does not apply to the parents of a disabled child, however.

Maximum period of leave per year

Under the fallback scheme, an employee may not take more than four weeks' parental leave in respect of any individual child during any one year. A year is the period of 12 months starting with the date on which the employee first became entitled (with the current employer) to take parental leave in respect of that child, and each successive period of 12 months.

Notice periods

The fallback scheme sets out certain requirements for employees to give notice of the dates on which they wish to take parental leave. The employee must give the employer at least 21 days' notice of the date on which he or she wishes the period of leave to begin, and also state the date when it will end.

Where the employee is the father of the child and the period of leave is to begin when the child is born, the notice:

- must specify the expected week of childbirth and how long the period of parental leave is to last, and
- must be given to the employer at least 21 days before the beginning of the expected week of childbirth.

Where parental leave is to begin on the date on which a child is placed with the employee for adoption, the notice:

- must specify the week in which the placement is expected to occur, and the duration of the period of leave requested, and
- must be given to the employer at least 21 days before the beginning of that week (or as soon as is reasonably practicable).

Postponement

Under the fallback scheme, an employer may postpone a period of parental leave in some circumstances. The employer cannot, however, postpone parental leave where the employee has given notice that he or she intends to start leave as soon as his or her child is born or on the date a child is placed with him or her for adoption. Apart from these two exceptions, the employer may postpone parental leave where the employee has given notice, but the employer considers that the operation of the business would be unduly disrupted if the employee took leave at the time requested.

In these circumstances, the employer must agree to allow the employee to take parental leave of the same length as the period requested within six months of the date on which the employee's leave would have begun if his or her request had been granted. The employer must give the employee written notice of the postponement, stating the reasons for it and specifying the dates between which parental leave may be taken. The notice must be given to the employee not more than seven days after the employee's notice was given to the employer.

CONTRACTUAL RIGHT TO PARENTAL LEAVE

Where an employee has both statutory and contractual rights to parental leave, then he or she may take advantage of whichever is the most favourable.

RECORD KEEPING

The law does not require employers to keep any specific records on parental leave. In most cases, however, it is likely that employers will want to do so:

- for management purposes
- so that they can demonstrate that they have given employees their statutory entitlement, and
- in order to be able to co-operate with other employers in providing information (on request) about how much parental leave an employee has already taken.

DETRIMENT AND DISMISSAL

Employees have the right not be subjected to any detriment for taking or seeking to take parental leave, and may complain to an employment tribunal if this happens. Where an employee is dismissed or selected for redundancy for taking parental leave, the dismissal will be automatically unfair.

ENFORCEMENT

Where an employer prevents or obstructs an employee from taking parental leave, or unreasonably postpones it, the employee may complain to an employment tribunal. The complaint must be made within three months of the date of the matter complained of. This deadline may be extended in cases where it is not reasonably practicable for the employee to present the complaint within three months. Where the tribunal finds the complaint well-founded, it will make a declaration to that effect and may award compensation to the employee. The amount of compensation will be what the tribunal considers just and equitable in all the circumstances, taking account of the employer's behaviour and any loss suffered by the employee.

BEST PRACTICE

Employers are free to design their own parental leave scheme as long as it at least complies with the regulations or is more generous. Employers who wish to create their own scheme will need to do so through a collective agreement, a workforce agreement or through agreement with each individual employee. In all cases, the agreement must:

- be in writing
- have effect for not more than five years

- be signed by the representatives of the workforce or of the particular group, or, if the employer employs 20 or fewer employees, either by the representatives or the majority of the employees.

Different arrangements may be made via the agreement about:
- notice of parental leave
- postponement of leave
- whether parental leave may be taken in blocks of more than four weeks, and/or in single days.

For example parental leave agreements could:
- apply to all parents, including, for example, those with less than one year's service, or those with children over five years old
- extend the total period of leave which can be taken above the 13-week statutory minimum
- be flexible, allowing for leave to be taken in a variety of ways
- guarantee that all employment rights (such as pension entitlement) will accrue and be preserved during parental leave
- be paid, in whole or in part
- guarantee the right to return to exactly the same job in all circumstances.

Where employers do not have their own scheme in place, they will be bound by the rules of the "fallback" scheme set out in the regulations. For information on the fallback scheme, see earlier in this chapter.

KEY FACTS

- An employee will be eligible for parental leave if he or she is the parent of, or has acquired formal parental responsibility for, a child under the age of five (under age 18 if the child is disabled), or has adopted a child under the age of 18.
- All periods of parental leave are unpaid unless the employer chooses to pay the employee full or part wage/salary whilst they are on leave.
- To qualify for parental leave, an employee must have at least one year's continuous service with his or her employer as at the date parental leave is to start.
- An employee who qualifies for parental leave is entitled to take a total of 13 weeks' leave in respect of each individual child (18 weeks' leave in respect of a child who is disabled).
- In most cases, parental leave may only be taken up until the child's fifth birthday.

- The parents of an adopted child may take leave up until the fifth anniversary of the date on which the child was placed with them for adoption (or the child's 18th birthday if that occurs sooner).
- Unless agreed otherwise through a relevant agreement, employees may not take parental leave in less than blocks of one week, except when the child is disabled (in which case each parent may choose to take parental leave in single days).
- An employee who wishes to take a period of parental leave must give his or her employer at least 21 days' notice, stating the dates on which the period of parental leave is to begin and end.
- Employees remain employed during periods of parental leave although most contractual terms, including pay, may be suspended.
- Employees must be permitted to return from parental leave on terms and conditions that are no less favourable than those that would have applied if they had not been absent.
- Employers and employees are free to agree their own parental leave schemes through collective, workforce or individual agreements, provided these contain certain key elements prescribed by statute and are incorporated into employees' contracts of employment.
- The Government's fallback scheme applies to employees who are not subject to a collective agreement, workforce agreement or individual agreement covering parental leave.
- The fallback scheme may modify provisions relating to minimum and maximum periods of parental leave, notice periods and postponement of the dates requested.
- Employees have the right not be dismissed or subjected to any detriment for taking or seeking to take parental leave.

CHAPTER 6

TIME OFF WORK TO CARE FOR DEPENDANTS

INTRODUCTION

All employees (both men and women) have the right, under s.57A of the **Employment Rights Act 1996**, to take a reasonable amount of unpaid time off work to deal with an unforeseen situation involving a dependant, and not to be dismissed or subjected to any detriment for doing so.

LEGAL REQUIREMENTS — A SUMMARY

The right to take unpaid time off work to care for dependants was implemented in order to ensure employees were permitted to take necessary time off work in circumstances where a dependant falls ill, is injured or assaulted, dies or gives birth, or in certain other defined circumstances. Although there is no set limit to the amount of time off that an employee may take, it was envisaged when the law was introduced that one or two days would be reasonable in most cases. This is because the right is intended to cover unforeseen matters and not those that can be planned for in advance.

ENTITLEMENT TO TIME OFF WORK TO CARE FOR DEPENDANTS

The right to take time off work to care for dependants applies to all employees irrespective of gender or family status. There is no minimum length of service required for an employee to acquire the right.

The right to time off is intended to cover unforeseen matters, ie those that are unexpected and occur suddenly and not circumstances in which an employee knows in advance that he or she is going to need time off for family reasons. Where employees do have advance knowledge that they are going to need time off, they may be able to apply for this as part of their holiday entitlement or as parental leave (if they are eligible) but would not, strictly speaking, qualify for the statutory right to take time off work to care for dependants.

How Much Time Off is Reasonable?

There is no set limit to the amount of time off that an employee may take to care for dependants, save that the time taken must be "reasonable". How much time off is reasonable will depend on individual circumstances. When deciding what is reasonable, a tribunal will consider what is reasonable to the employee, given his or her circumstances and discount any inconvenience to the employer.

The Department of Trade and Industry (DTI) suggests that one or two days would normally be sufficient for an employee to deal with a family emergency and, if necessary, to make alternative arrangements for the continuing care of the dependant. The actual circumstances of each case should, however, be considered on their own merits.

There is no statutory right for an employee to be paid during time off to care for dependants, and this matter is therefore left to the employer's discretion.

Definition of "Dependant"

A "dependant" in relation to the right to time off means:
- the employee's spouse or partner
- one of the employee's children
- one of the employee's parents
- someone who lives in the same household as the employee (but not his or her employee, tenant, lodger or boarder)
- someone who would rely on the employee for assistance in the event of illness, injury or assault (which could occur, for example, where an employee cares for a neighbour and this person falls ill unexpectedly).

A dependant does not, therefore, have to be related to the employee.

Circumstances in which Time Off may be Taken

Circumstances where an employee may take time off include:

- to provide assistance when a dependant falls ill, gives birth or is injured or assaulted (including mental illness)
- to make arrangements for the provision of care when a dependant is ill or injured
- when a dependant dies
- when a dependant gives birth
- to cope when the arrangements for caring for a dependant unexpectedly break down (for example, if an employee's childminder calls in sick)
- to deal with an unexpected incident involving the employee's child when the child is at school.

The right to time off work to care for dependants is not intended to cover bereavement leave in the event that a close relative of the employee dies. The EAT ruled in *Forster v Cartwright Black Solicitors* [2004] IRLR 781 that the right to time off in consequence of the death of a dependant is restricted to the time off that is necessary for the employee to deal with the direct consequences of the death, for example the need to deal with legal matters and time to arrange and attend the funeral.

Equally, the right does not permit employees repeatedly to take time off work in respect of a dependant who has a chronic or recurring medical condition and who therefore needs care on a regular basis. In these circumstances, the need for care is foreseeable and not unexpected. The right is for the employee to take time off work in order to make the necessary arrangements for the dependant's long-term care, rather than to provide such care personally on every occasion it is required (see *Qua v John Ford Morrison Solicitors* [2003] IRLR 184).

Employees' Notice Requirements

The employee is only entitled to time off to care for dependants if he or she tells the employer:
- the reason for the absence, as soon as is reasonably practicable, and
- how long the absence is expected to last (except in cases where the employee is not able to inform the employer about the absence until he or she is back at work).

Notice does not have to be given in writing.

If an employee does not comply with the notification requirements, the employer may treat the absence as unauthorised leave.

DETRIMENT AND DISMISSAL

Employees must not be subjected to any detriment for reasons relating to time off to care for dependants, and, if this happens, they may complain to an employment tribunal.

Similarly, if an employee is dismissed or selected for redundancy for any reason connected with the fact they took time off work to care for dependants, the dismissal will be automatically unfair. No qualifying period of service is needed to bring a claim for unfair dismissal in these circumstances, and no upper age limit applies.

ENFORCEMENT

Where an employee is unreasonably refused time off to care for dependants, then he or she may complain to an employment tribunal. The complaint must be made within three months of the date when the employer refused time off. In cases where it was not reasonably practicable for the complaint to be presented within three months, the tribunal may extend the period as it considers reasonable.

Where a tribunal decides that the complaint is well-founded, it will make a declaration to that effect and may award the employee compensation. The amount of compensation will be such as the tribunal considers just and equitable in all the circumstances, taking into account the employer's fault and the employee's loss.

SAMPLE POLICY

Caring for Dependants Policy and Procedure

Policy

The Organisation recognises that employees may at some stage in their working lives be responsible for and committed to the care of a dependant and that this could potentially affect their ability to attend work. Where such a situation arises, the Organisation offers practical support through its Dependants Leave Scheme.

Procedure

1. All employees are entitled to up to _____ days' paid/unpaid absence per year as leave for the care of a dependant. This is in addition to annual leave and other absence entitlements.

2. Dependant leave may be granted for pressing and important family reasons such as bereavement, illness of a close family member and other family emergencies.
3. Requests for dependant leave must be made to _____. Wherever possible, such requests should be made in writing and in advance. Where the reason for the request is the illness of a close family member, the employee may be asked to produce a medical certificate.
4. The Organisation will grant employees dependant leave on the basis of what is reasonable in all the circumstances. However, not more than _____ days' dependant leave per annum will be paid.

KEY FACTS

- The right to take time off work to care for dependants applies to all employees irrespective of gender, family status or length of service.
- The right to time off is intended to cover unforeseen matters, ie those that are unexpected and occur suddenly and not circumstances in which an employee knows in advance that he or she is going to need time off for family reasons.
- There is no set limit to the amount of time off that an employee may take to care for dependants, save that the time taken must be "reasonable".
- There is no statutory right for an employee to be paid during time off to care for dependants, and this matter is therefore left to the employer's discretion.
- A "dependant" is specifically defined in the legislation.
- Circumstances where an employee may take time off are specifically defined in the legislation.
- Employees have the right not be dismissed or subjected to any detriment because they have taken time off to care for dependants.

CHAPTER 7

OTHER TYPES OF LEAVE

INTRODUCTION

Irrespective of the statutory right for employees to take time off to care for dependants (see Chapter 6), employers may choose to have their own more generous policies that grant employees time off work in a wider range of situations and possibly with pay. Such policies may cover compassionate leave and/or other types of personal leave, together with career breaks. These will be contractual benefits, the precise terms of which will depend on the policy itself, the terms of the employee's contract and whether the leave is stated to be an absolute right or at management's discretion.

COMPASSIONATE LEAVE

Many employers choose to adopt a policy of granting paid compassionate leave to employees in certain circumstances. Devising and implementing a clear policy on compassionate leave will assist the employer in ensuring consistency and fairness of treatment for employees in different parts of the organisation. Irrespective of the circumstances defined in s.57A of the **Employment Rights Act 1996** as being grounds for time off to care for dependants (including the death or unexpected illness of a dependant), compassionate leave would normally be granted in circumstances where a close member of the employee's family, or even a close friend, became seriously ill or died. There may be other events for which employers may consider granting compassionate leave such as for an employee experiencing a divorce, marital difficulties, difficulties involving relationships with children, etc. In theory, any event in an employee's personal life that is causing severe distress may be worthy of compassionate leave.

It is a fact of working life that employees (especially those who work full time) sometimes need time off work to deal with a wide range of personal matters, including many which cannot be anticipated. Employees who are denied time off, made to feel guilty for asking for time off, or coerced into returning to work before a personal problem has been properly resolved, are unlikely to be motivated or productive workers. They may also suffer undue stress as a result of pressure placed on them by their employer to attend work, or fear that their job will be under threat if they take time off. An unsympathetic employer may then find that an employee denied time off for personal reasons produces a doctor's certificate stating that he or she is unfit to attend work due to stress. Thus the employer will end up having no option but to accede to the employee's need for time off — but in these circumstances it will have been achieved at the expense of the employee's good will, commitment and trust.

A good employer will adopt the attitude that it is appropriate to support employees who are experiencing genuine family or personal problems. Support will involve granting time off work within reason so that the employee can deal with the problem and come to terms with the distress which the personal problems may be causing. It is up to each individual employer to decide whether such time off should be paid or unpaid, or a combination of both.

Devising a Policy on Compassionate Leave

When devising a policy on compassionate leave, it is recommended that employers should, as a starting point, consider the definition of dependants used in the **Employment Rights Act 1996**. This includes the employee's spouse or partner, children, parents, any other dependant who lives in the same household and anyone else who would rely on the employee for assistance in the event that he or she was ill, injured or assaulted.

The employer may, however, wish to extend the provision of compassionate leave beyond those dependants defined in statute. Many people have very close relationships with (for example) their grandparents or grandchildren. It is recommended that any company policy on compassionate leave should clearly define which relatives "qualify" an employee to take time off on account of their death or serious illness. These could include:

- spouse or partner
- child
- parent
- brother and sister
- aunt and uncle
- grandparent
- grandchild
- parents, brothers, sisters, sons and daughters in law.

It is also up to each employer to decide whether or not to pay employees all or part of their normal level of pay while they are absent on compassionate leave. There may be an express term in the employees' contract giving the right to paid compassionate leave up to a fixed number of days, or such a term may be implied through custom and practice.

Normally a certain amount of discretion in terms of the number of days off is recommended so that the employer may show consideration to an employee in times of difficulty. One employee may need several days off to make complex funeral arrangements at the opposite end of the country, whilst another may require only one day off to attend a funeral.

As in other areas of conferring employee benefits, it is important that any discretionary arrangements are applied fairly and consistently, while still taking into account the needs of the individual employee. Guidelines for managers should be devised in order to avoid the situation arising where one line manager may adopt a sympathetic approach to an employee who requests time off, while another takes the view that as little time off as possible should be granted.

Time off Work to Cope with Personal/Family Difficulties

Employers may wish to consider granting a reasonable amount of paid time off work to employees in a range of other situations. These might include:

- divorce, separation or other serious marital difficulties
- problems with a partner or child who is in trouble with the law
- dealing with a child who has become involved with drugs
- caring for a child who has a long-term medical condition or illness which flares up from time to time.

Employees who wish to attend counselling or marriage guidance may not be able to schedule appointments outside their working hours and so time off work would be essential to allow them to receive the necessary support. In such circumstances it would be reasonable for the employer to grant employees time off work, and not to penalise them in any way on account of the fact that they needed such time off.

A reasonable employer will understand that such circumstances inevitably occur from time to time, and that the best approach is to support the employee in granting them, within reason, whatever time off they require even if this causes inconvenience to the business.

Time off Work to Care for a Sick Child

Women sometimes experience discrimination in employment on account of a belief or perception that they are likely to take excessive time off work to care for their children when they are sick. It is of course a fact of life that children become sick from time to time, and it would be unreasonable for any employer to expect an employee with children not to encounter the occasional need for time off work, in particular if a child has a long-term illness or disability. This need will, of course, affect both men and women, and would be especially likely in the event of the employee being a single parent.

Where a child falls ill suddenly or is injured or assaulted, the employee has the statutory right to take a reasonable amount of unpaid time off work to care for the child, or to make arrangements for their care (see Chapter 6). There may, however, be non-emergency situations that do not, strictly speaking, entitle the employee to take time off but may nevertheless necessitate such time off from a practical perspective. No employee can, or should be expected to, choose between their children and their work and any employer that adopts such an approach will inevitably find that morale and motivation suffer, working relationships break down and performance deteriorates.

In contrast, employees who know that they have the genuine support of their employer in times of difficulty are more likely to feel motivated to make the necessary arrangements for the care of their child promptly and return to work as soon as possible. There is also a good chance that employees who are treated in accordance with such positive policies, will, once they have returned to work, put in extra effort to make up for the time away from work.

It is recommended, therefore, that employers should:

84

- adopt a positive and supportive approach towards employees who need to take time off work to care for a sick child
- ensure that no employee feels pressurised to remain at work at a time when he or she is feeling distressed or worried about a child
- ensure no employee is made to feel guilty about needing to take time off work in circumstances where a child is sick
- wherever possible, grant time off with pay over and above annual holiday entitlement, provided the amount of time taken off is not excessive or unreasonable.

SAMPLE POLICY

Compassionate Leave Policy and Procedure

Policy
Compassionate leave is intended to allow employees to take time off work on the occurrence of the death or serious illness of a close family member, or in the case of some other event that is causing serious personal disruption or distress to the employee.

Procedure
For the purposes of paid compassionate leave, "close family member" is restricted to the following: spouse/partner, parent, sister/brother, child, grandparent and grandchild.

The amount of time off granted is discretionary, and will normally be from one to three days. In exceptional circumstances, up to five days' leave may be granted. Compassionate leave will be paid at the employee's normal basic rate of pay (exclusive of overtime, shift allowance, bonus, commission, etc).

Further time off may be granted without pay if the employee is experiencing a major family or personal problem.

CAREER BREAKS

Many employers operate policies whereby they grant employees career breaks, ie breaks from employment for a pre-determined or flexible period of time, usually between six months and a few years. During the career break, the employer and employee keep in touch by a variety of means and the employee is given a guarantee that a job will be available when he or she is ready to return to work. Increasingly, employers see the advantages in making career breaks available to both male and female employees who need to care for their children or a dependant or disabled relative. Some employers may also offer career breaks for the purpose of undertaking a university degree course or college course (usually known as a sabbatical) or even time off to allow an employee to pursue a personal interest, undertake research or travel abroad.

Agreements for career breaks vary and may be formal or informal. More formal arrangements specify particular terms and conditions and include keeping-in-touch schemes and work assignments. Re-entry schemes guarantee a return to a job at the same level at which the person left. Retainer schemes place people on a waiting list until a suitable vacancy arises at the level at which they left.

Advantages and Disadvantages of Offering Career Breaks

Advantages
- Employers can enhance returns on investment in staff knowledge, skills and training by attracting valued employees back to work, who would otherwise be lost to the organisation.
- Recruitment and training costs are likely to be reduced.
- Employees can be encouraged to pursue higher education courses which, if a career break scheme did not exist, they may not otherwise have the opportunity to pursue.
- The existence of a career break scheme can enhance the public image of an employer, and make it more attractive to potential job applicants.

Disadvantages
- The cost implications of the initial development of a scheme can act as a barrier.
- The question of continuity of employment can be a difficult one.
- If the employer makes a firm guarantee that it will re-employ the employee after the career break, this could cause problems in recessionary times when other staff are being made redundant.
- In highly specialised, rapidly changing work environments a long break may not be feasible, as information and jobs change very quickly.

The Law and Career Breaks

There is no statutory entitlement for any employee to take a career break. Employees' rights to time off for family-related reasons are restricted to the leave available as maternity leave, paternity leave, adoption leave and/or parental leave. Increasingly, however, employers are choosing to make provision for employees to take career breaks, provided the reason for doing so is an appropriate one. It is common, for example, for career breaks to be taken immediately after maternity leave, and in the higher education world for employees to take a sabbatical for the purposes of research and/or travel.

The practice of allowing such employment breaks gives rise to two linked legal issues which, if not addressed before the employee's break commences, can create uncertainty regarding the employee's employment status and statutory entitlements in the future:

- whether continuous employment for the purposes of the **Employment Rights Act 1996** is broken
- the continued existence of the employee's contract of employment during the break.

Both issues can be of considerable complexity and are examined below.

Continuity of Employment

The length of an employee's continuous employment is important because a number of statutory rights (for example entitlement to statutory redundancy pay) depend on length of service. However, computing continuous service becomes complicated where there has been a break in an employee's career. The employee's continuous employment may have been broken by a career break or may be deemed to have continued.

Presumption of continuity

Under the **Employment Rights Act 1996**, an employee's period of employment is presumed to be unbroken unless the contrary is shown. However, continuity will be broken where there has been a gap of at least one calendar week between two separate contracts of employment. The gap must include a period from a Sunday to a Saturday inclusive. There are, however, situations in which continuity can be preserved despite a gap of more than a week between two contracts of employment.

During an employee's career break, there are three possible arrangements regarding the contract of employment.

1. The employee's contract of employment continues during the career break.
2. The employee's contract of employment terminates but he or she remains on the employer's books.
3. The employee's contract of employment terminates at the start of the career break.

If the contract continues during the break
If the employee's contract remains in force during a career break, the position is clear — continuity is preserved. This is the case irrespective of the actual hours worked (if any) during a particular week, because a week will count in any event if it is covered by a contract of employment. The same principle will apply if the employee is paid full or part salary during the career break — even a small retainer will mean that continuity is preserved.

If the employee's contract of employment terminates but he or she remains on the employer's books
Section 212(3)(c) of the **Employment Rights Act 1996** allows periods during which there is no contract of employment in existence to count towards continuous employment if the absence from work was as a result of an arrangement made in advance or custom. This means that, once an employee has returned to work after an agreed career break, the period of the gap will count towards their period of continuous service. Thus if the employee remains "on the employer's books" during the career break, it is likely that continuity will be preserved.

If the employee's contract of employment terminates at the start of the career break
In these circumstances, the question of whether the employee's contract will later be deemed to have continued in force during the career break will depend on whether or not there was an "arrangement" by which it was agreed in advance that the employee would definitely return to work. Where the employee is guaranteed re-employment within a defined time-scale, it is likely that continuity will be preserved. By contrast, where the employee is simply told that he or she may re-apply for employment in the future, perhaps with their application receiving favourable treatment, then no arrangement will exist and continuity will not be preserved during the break.

Continued Existence of the Employee's Contract

Where an employee takes a career break, the continuing nature of the contractual relationship between employer and employee depends entirely on what has been agreed between them, whether expressly or impliedly.

The normal practice will be an express agreement for the termination of the existing contract, with an arrangement that the employee will return to the same job (or a similar job) on a new contract at an agreed future date. In these circumstances, the employee's entitlement to contractual benefits will cease upon commencement of the break. It may be, however, that some residual obligations under the contract remain in force; for example, there may be a requirement for the employee to attend an annual training event, conduct some research work while on leave or stay in touch with the employer at defined intervals. These requirements would need to be clearly set down in writing to avoid confusion at a later date.

Where no agreement is reached, the nature of the contractual relationship will have to be implied according to the intent of the parties at the commencement of the break. What can be implied will depend on the circumstances. The outcome of any dispute on this matter will be uncertain and employers should therefore not allow an employee to take a career break without express agreement on what (if any) contractual rights will continue during the period of the career break.

Other Legal Issues

Schemes must be made available to both men and women in order to avoid breach of the **Sex Discrimination Act 1975**.

Where career breaks are offered to full-time employees in defined circumstances, the same benefit must be offered to comparable part-time employees. This is because the **Part-time Workers (Prevention of Less Favourable Treatment) Regulations 2000** prevent employers from treating part-time employees less favourably than equivalent full-time employees on the grounds of their part-time status.

In light of the **Employment Equality (Age) Regulations 2006**, implemented in October 2006, employers should not use age as a criterion in determining who is eligible for career breaks.

Any length of service provision applied in respect of eligibility for career breaks should be considered carefully, as using length of service as a criterion in determining employees' benefits will discriminate indirectly against younger staff. The Regulations provide, however, that benefits that are made dependent on employees' length of service are automatically permitted if the length of service criterion is five years or less. Longer service requirements on the other hand require justification, ie the employer would have to be able to show that the length of service provision fulfilled a defined business need.

Contractual Issues

Employers adopting a policy of allowing staff to take career breaks should be able to avoid the difficulties that may otherwise arise through contractual/statutory interpretation by devising and implementing a career break scheme. A career break scheme should tackle two issues:
- the basis on which application for leave is made and granted
- the terms of employment, if any, during the career break.

The basis on which application for leave is made and granted
The employer's policy should clearly define the grounds on which application may be made for a career break. The grounds could include:
- childcare
- care of an elderly, sick or disabled relative
- study or training
- research
- travel
- setting up a business (provided the business in question would be relevant to or useful for the employer).

The decision-making process should be made clear. Reference should be made to the criteria on which the decision to grant or refuse leave will be made, including:
- the employer's operational requirements
- the reason for requesting leave
- whether the scheme is to be open to all staff, and if not which staff are eligible
- the minimum length of service required by an employee to be eligible for a career break, typically ranging from one to five years
- (possibly) the employee's general disciplinary record.

The procedure should also set out how far in advance of the start of the career break the employee should apply and to whom an application should be made.

Employees whose request for a career break is refused should have the opportunity to raise a formal internal grievance challenging the decision, and to have the grievance heard by a senior member of management.

The terms of employment, if any, during the career break
A policy on career breaks should clarify all the following points:
- the minimum and maximum lengths of any career break
- the status of an employee's contract of employment during the career break
- whether any terms of employment or mutual obligations will continue during the break, and if so what these are
- whether the employee will receive any pay during the career break
- in respect of any benefits calculated by reference to length of service, how the period of the career break will affect entitlement to those benefits
- how any occupational pension benefits will be affected — usually these contractual benefits will cease to be applicable and will not accrue during the break
- whether and how the employee is expected to keep in touch with the employer during the career break
- whether the employee may take up paid employment elsewhere during the career break
- the minimum period of notice that the employee must give the employer prior to returning to work (normally at least three months)
- what training/induction will be provided at re-entry, for example refresher courses or project work
- who will have overall responsibility for the scheme.

Staying in Touch

Employees are usually required to stay in touch with the employer during their career break. The contact established and continued by both employer and employee during the break from work is a key factor in its success. It provides proof of the ongoing interest by the employer in retaining the skills of the individual and also of the interest by the individual in eventually returning to work. It helps to maintain an employee's confidence, skills and knowledge and by doing so eases the return to work process.

Working and Training During a Career Break

Many career break schemes provide for a minimum period of work that the employee must do for the employer during each year of the career break. This is part of keeping in touch and helps to demonstrate the commitment of the employee to return eventually as a permanent member of staff. Naturally the timing and arrangements for this period of work need to be agreed well in advance.

Training while on career break may be very important in order to ensure the employee's skills are kept up to date. In particular, for employees involved in highly skilled occupations where technology is rapidly changing, training will be very important, both from a practical point of view and psychologically. Training should be planned well ahead in order that the employee on the break can, if necessary, make adequate care arrangements for dependant children or other relatives.

Working Elsewhere during a Career Break

The question of whether an employee on a career break may take up paid work elsewhere should be addressed and agreed before the break commences. For some employers this may not be an important issue as they may take the view that they are offering a break in employment and what happens in this time is up to the individual. To other employers, it is of great importance because they feel that they have first call on the individual's time and skills and there may even be a question of confidential knowledge going outside the company.

The terms of the career break scheme should state clearly that, where the employee obtains alternative employment without the employer's consent, the employer will have the right to terminate the career break arrangement (and the contract of employment, if that contract is continuing) without notice.

The employer may, however, wish to consider permitting voluntary (unpaid) work as the experience gained from such work may be valuable for the employee and is unlikely to interfere with the main employment.

Returning to Work

An agreement allowing the employee to take a career break should set out arrangements in anticipation of and in preparation for their return. Provisions that may be incorporated into the scheme include the following:

- the extent to which the right to return to work is guaranteed, ie is there an absolute guarantee, or is the employer agreeing to offer the employee a job only if/when one becomes available
- whether the employee is entitled to return to the same job, at the same grade and level and under the same contractual terms as before, or if the employer can place him or her in a different position at a suitable level
- what will happen if the employee's original job has disappeared, for example as a result of a reorganisation or redundancy programme
- whether the employer maintains the right to require the employee to attend refresher courses with a view to maintaining skills
- provision for retraining and re-entry to the working environment (including payment for attendance on training and refresher courses)
- a requirement that the employee notify the employer if the return date is to be postponed, that the reason for late return be given, and that a doctor's certificate be provided if the reason is illness.

The employer should ensure that any guarantee of re-employment is carefully worded so as to avoid any ambiguity or challenge at a later date.

SAMPLE POLICY

Career Break Policy and Procedure

Policy
The Organisation may, at its discretion and subject to certain conditions, allow employees to take a career break and return to work afterwards. A career break may be granted for the following purposes:
- *childcare or dependant care*
- *research*
- *study at university or college*
- *overseas travel*
- *any other reason that is agreed between the employer and the employee.*

Procedure
The career break scheme will be open to all employees who have a minimum of [ ] years' service, including part-time employees.

The Organisation reserves the right to make the final decision on whether to grant an employee a career break and the length of the career break. Whether a career break is granted will depend on many factors, including the needs of the business at the time in question.

The conditions applicable to career breaks are as follows.

- A career break may be any period of time of between six months and [ ] years.
- The employee will be required to resign before the start of the career break, thus bringing all normal contractual benefits to an end.
- Career breaks will be unpaid.
- Accrual of pension benefits will cease during a career break.
- The employee must use up any accrued holiday entitlement for the current holiday year prior to starting their career break.
- Subject to the next point, at the end of the agreed period of the career break the employee will be guaranteed re-employment in a job at the same grade and level and on equivalent terms as the job he or she held prior to the start of the career break. There is, however, no guarantee that the individual can be offered exactly the same job as he or she occupied before the career break.
- If exceptional circumstances have occurred during the period of the career break involving (for example) a major reorganisation, a take-over or large-scale redundancies, it may not be possible for the Organisation to re-employ the individual at the end of the career break.
- For the purposes of service-related contractual benefits, the employee's length of service prior to the career break and their service after the break will be added together, whilst the period of the career break itself will not count towards length of service for contractual purposes or seniority.
- Once the individual has returned to work, his or her length of service for statutory purposes will be regarded as continuous (as required by the provisions of the **Employment Rights Act 1996**).
- During the period of the career break, the individual will be required to keep in touch with the Organisation at regular intervals, details of which will be agreed with the individual.
- During the career break, the Organisation will offer the individual the opportunity to attend any relevant training that is taking place. It is a condition of the career break scheme that the individual agrees to attend a minimum of [ ] days' training in each year of the career break if asked to do so. The Organisation will meet all costs associated with this training.
- The individual will not be permitted to take up any other paid employment during a career break, although voluntary unpaid work may be undertaken with the Organisation's permission.

- The individual will be given any necessary refresher training on re-employment, the details of which will be agreed at the time.
- If the individual wishes to return to work with the Organisation before the planned end of the career break, he or she must give a minimum of three months' notice of the proposed return date.
- If the individual is unable to return to work at the end of the career break, he or she must notify the Organisation in writing giving the reason and, if the reason is illness, provide a doctor's certificate.

If an employee acts in breach of any of the conditions of the career break scheme, or fails to return to work by the pre-arranged date, the career break arrangement will terminate immediately and the right to be offered re-employment will be lost. In the event of illness, the Organisation will, at its discretion, allow an extension to the career break period of up to [ ] months.

KEY FACTS

- Irrespective of the statutory right for employees to take time off to care for dependants, employers may choose to have their own more generous policies that grant employees time off work in a wider range of situations and possibly with pay.
- Devising and implementing a clear policy on compassionate leave will assist the employer in ensuring consistency and fairness of treatment for employees in different parts of the organisation.
- It is up to each employer to decide whether or not to pay an employee all or part of their normal level of pay whilst they are absent on compassionate leave.
- A certain amount of discretion in terms of the number of days off is usually recommended so that the employer may show consideration to an employee in times of difficulty.
- It is important that any discretionary arrangements on compassionate leave are applied fairly and consistently, therefore guidelines for managers should be devised.
- Employers should adopt a positive and supportive approach towards employees who have the need to take time off work to care for a sick child.
- There is no statutory entitlement for any employee to take a career break, although many employers choose to make provision for career breaks.

- A career break during which there is no contract of employment in force may still count towards an employee's continuous employment for statutory purposes if the absence was as a result of an arrangement or custom.
- Where an employee takes a career break, the continuing nature of the contractual relationship between employer and employee depends entirely on what has been agreed between them.
- Where an employer operates a career break scheme, this must be available on an equal footing to both men and women, and to both full-time and part-time employees.
- A career break scheme should clearly define the grounds on which application may be made for a career break, which may include (for example) childcare or elderly dependant care, study or research.
- There are many factors that will need to be clarified in respect of the terms applicable to an employee's career break, including in particular, the maximum length of the break and whether any terms of employment or mutual obligations will continue, and if so what these are.
- A career break scheme should define clearly how the employee should keep in touch with the employer and whether or not he or she is permitted to do any other work during the period of the break.
- The employer will need to define clearly what the individual's right will be in respect of returning to work, ie whether he or she is guaranteed re-employment in the same job, or a similar job at the same level, or whether the commitment is simply to offer a position as and when one becomes available.

CHAPTER 8

CHILDCARE AND DEPENDANT CARE

INTRODUCTION

Employers in the UK are increasingly becoming aware of the need for better childcare provision. Women comprise over 40% of the workforce and many will only be able to work if they have access to affordable childcare. The availability of appropriate and good quality childcare is therefore one of the most important forms of support that an employer can offer working parents.

PROVISION OF CHILDCARE

Women are more likely now than at any time in the recent past to return to work after the birth of a child. Where this is the case, workplace or employer sponsored nurseries, holiday play-schemes, childcare allowances or vouchers and after-school care can all play a part in simplifying working arrangements. The availability of such benefits for prospective employees will give the employer a competitive advantage over other employers in the quest to recruit and retain talented people. Lack of provision of childcare facilities on the other hand will result in the loss of competent female employees (since it is women who generally have most of the responsibility for childcare) who may elect to take time out of work altogether when their children are young, or may only be able to work part-time or on short-term contracts.

A TUC Guide (*Who's Looking after the Children? A Trade Union Guide to Negotiating Childcare*, available at *www.tuc.org.uk*), claims that employers could do more to assist working parents with childcare, often at no great cost. The Guide suggests a number of ways in which employers could support employees in this area, including:

- providing a workplace nursery that offers discounted places to their employees
- joining forces with other employers to provide a crèche for their employees
- providing childcare vouchers or childcare subsidies
- allowing parents to change their hours to fit in with the drop-off and pick-up times of the nurseries they use.

The Guide claims that "the business case for providing some form of childcare support for employee is overwhelming".

Sex Discrimination against Women with Childcare Responsibilities

The difficulties of combining paid employment with responsibility for childcare are to some extent recognised in law under the **Sex Discrimination Act 1975**. Although the Act does not give an express right to work part time, or move from full-time to part time working, a refusal to agree to a woman's request to work part-time could lead to a claim for indirect sex discrimination. Courts and tribunals have for many years accepted the general principle that fewer women than men are able to work full time because of childcare commitments. Unless the employer can justify the requirement for an individual to work full time (as opposed to part time or as part of a job-share), then it is likely that a woman who suffers a disadvantage as a result would succeed in a claim for indirect sex discrimination.

Other Legal Provisions

The **Part-time Workers (Prevention of Less Favourable Treatment) Regulations 2000** also give protection to both men and women who do in fact work part-time by prohibiting unfavourable treatment on grounds of part-time status. Protection applies in relation to both contractual terms and non-contractual benefits, such as access to training and promotion.

There is also the right to request flexible working, available to employees who have parental responsibility for a child under six years old. This is dealt with fully in Chapter 10.

EMPLOYER INITIATIVES AND TAX TREATMENT

There is no legal requirement for employers to provide financial help with childcare but there are tax concessions aimed at encouraging employers to do so. Financial help can be provided in two main ways:
- workplace nurseries
- childcare allowances and vouchers.

Workplace Nurseries — Tax Treatment

Although the payment by the employer of an employee's childcare costs or the provision of vouchers to enable an employee to purchase childcare is generally taxable, the provision of childcare is specifically exempted from tax if certain conditions are satisfied. The **Finance Act 1990** introduced a limited exemption from a benefit in kind charge on employer-provided nursery care facilities. This means that employees are exempted from income tax on the benefit of nurseries provided by their employers either at the workplace or elsewhere on the employer's premises. Domestic premises are excluded. Nurseries jointly run with other employers, voluntary bodies or local authorities are included, provided the premises are owned by one or more of those employers. Thus if an employer provided a trained nursery nurse to look after several children on the employer's premises, the benefit would be exempt. In contrast, if the children were looked after in one of the employee's homes, the benefit would be taxable.

Similar facilities provided for older children after school or during school holidays are also exempt. It is a condition of the exemption that the childcare facilities must comply with any legal requirement for registration by the appropriate local authority. The child must be a child of the employee, or must live with or be maintained by the employee.

The question of tax treatment is an important one given the Government's objective of creating a national childcare strategy. Tax relief is currently confined to workplace nurseries but there are proposals to extend this benefit to include all forms of registered childcare provision paid for by an employer.

Childcare facilities can be beneficial to both employer and employee. The employee can continue working, knowing that his or her child is being cared for safely in a convenient and close location. The employer has the advantage of retaining staff who otherwise might be forced to leave in order to look after their children. Practical considerations may, however, prevent many employers from taking up this option.

Childcare Allowances and Vouchers

Where nursery provision is not practicable, some employers may wish to provide childcare allowances to their employees. A childcare allowance may take the form of a cash allowance paid to an individual employee along with salary, or a payment to an intermediary childcare fund. Unlike the provision of a workplace nursery, this benefit is liable to income tax.

A better approach for employers who wish to provide their staff with childcare benefits is to consider:

- contracting directly with a registered or approved childcare provider for the provision of childcare, or
- providing childcare vouchers to employees.

Since April 2005, directly contracted childcare provision by the employer has been exempt from income tax and National Insurance contributions, now up to a maximum of £55 per employee per week. Both parents may claim this exemption from their respective employers.

Certain rules and conditions must be met if the £55 per week childcare provision is to be free of income tax and National Insurance.

- The care provided must be "qualifying childcare". This includes care provided by registered childminders, nurseries, play schemes, out-of-hours clubs run by a school or local authority and childcare schemes run by approved providers. Care provided by the employee's partner or a relative of the child in the employee's home will not qualify for the tax exemption.
- The childcare under the scheme must be available to all employees of the employer, or to all those at a particular location.
- The child in respect of whom vouchers are provided must be the employee's child or stepchild, or one who resides with the employee in circumstances where the employee has parental responsibility for the child and maintains him or her.
- The child must be under 16 years of age.

Childcare vouchers provided by the employer to the employee are also specifically exempt from income tax and National Insurance contributions up to £55 per employee per week (or £243 per employee per month). The vouchers may be produced and administered by the employer, or obtained from a voucher company. They can be used to pay for most forms of childcare including care provided by registered childminders, nurseries, after-school schemes and holiday schemes.

To qualify for the tax exemption, the vouchers must:

- be used only for qualifying childcare

- be provided under a scheme that is open to all employees, or to all those at a particular location
- be used to enable employees to obtain care for a child under 16 years of age.

One matter which employers may wish to draw to employees' attention is that if childcare vouchers are provided under a "salary sacrifice scheme", the employee's entitlement (if any) to child tax credit and working tax credit may be reduced. This is because the vouchers will have the effect of reducing the employee's actual childcare costs on which the tax credits are calculated.

These forms of assistance offer the employer the advantage of not involving the capital costs that may be associated with a workplace nursery. They are also more flexible as they can provide equally for employees who live at a distance from the workplace (and who may therefore be out of range for a workplace nursery) and for those who live close by. The disadvantage of vouchers is that they do not guarantee that quality childcare support is available to parents, although they will go some way to alleviating financial pressures.

Before paying an allowance, contracting childcare provision directly or providing vouchers, employers must decide how much they can afford. A survey of the existing workforce and how many employees have children under 16 can give an estimate of the cost in the first year of introduction. These costs could increase if childcare provision is used as a recruitment tool.

Local social services departments can provide employers with estimates of the average childminder and nursery charges within the area so that an employer can accurately estimate what the cost would be of contracting childcare provision directly and what percentage of the actual costs of childcare the employer could afford to pay.

BEST PRACTICE

Employers may consider a range of options to support employees who have childcare responsibilities ranging from workplace nurseries, childcare allowances and vouchers to providing information about childcare. The option that an employer chooses will depend on the context of their operations and the needs of their employees.

Employers and Childcare Provision for the Under Fives

Whilst many parents may prefer to use a nursery, their choice will be influenced not only by availability, but also by cost, location and quality of provision. A workplace nursery may be an expensive benefit to provide and its effectiveness depends upon the availability of a convenient location, one which is not too costly and which offers practicable travel to work arrangements for parents. Workplace nurseries have traditionally been most common in the public sector and in some of the larger organisations within the private sector.

Employers and Childcare Provision for the Over Fives

It is often assumed that as children become older and start school, childcare problems for parents diminish. In fact they can often increase, as the school day is shorter than the usual working day and school holidays are vastly longer than most employees' holiday entitlements. Employees are typically granted about five weeks annual holiday, but school holidays last for about 13 weeks in total. There are therefore about eight weeks when children may be at home while parents have to be at work. Even in a two-parent family, if the leave of both parents were to be taken separately, there is still a gap of about three weeks when school and work patterns do not balance. A term-time work arrangement is one way of overcoming this imbalance (see Chapter 9 — *Flexible Working Patterns*).

CASE STUDIES

Case Study 1 — HSBC Bank plc

HSBC Bank plc is one of the leading providers of nursery places for its staff. Its interest commenced with an attempt at the end of the 1980s to reduce staff turnover. Wastage was high and this encouraged growing interest in nursery provision, particularly in order to retain women after a period of maternity leave. By 1997 the Midland Bank (the predecessor of the HSBC Bank) provided over 900 nursery places for employees across the country. However, the majority of these places resulted from partnership arrangements which proved to be a practical way of increasing day-care provision for the under fives (*Encouraging Employers: Commercial Sector Business Survey, London and the South-East*. Working for Childcare, 1997).

In 1988, prior to the introduction of its Childcare Programme, 70% of the bank's maternity leavers did not return to work — the retention figure was 30%. In 2002, HSBC was in its fourteenth year of the nursery programme and the retention figure had significantly improved to 85%.

Case Study 2 — Partnership Provision of Day Care for the Under Fives

The following examples, just some of those cited by Working for Childcare, highlight the variety and the innovative nature of some of the initiatives.

Leeds City Council coordinated a child-minding network which includes Leeds Metropolitan University, BT Mobile, Leeds University, Leeds TEC, Department of Health and Benefits Office, Leeds General Infirmary, ASDA and Leeds Council. Kingston Council, in partnership with the Metropolitan Police, set up two "Kidsenters" run on a franchise basis. Milton Keynes Council's Community and Economic Development Department developed nurseries in partnership with HSBC, the Open University and BT. Partners supplied the premises and employers paid for the number of places which they needed.

CARING FOR OTHER DEPENDANTS

Despite the right to request flexible working being introduced (in April 2007) for employees who care for dependant relatives (see chapter 10), most employers have yet to introduce support for employees who look after frail, disabled or ill dependants of any age. The business case for doing so is every bit as valid as that for supporting employees with caring responsibilities for children: the high cost of recruiting and training new employees makes retention of existing staff vital. Juggling paid work and caring responsibilities without support from an employer can prove so difficult that some carers feel they have no option but to give up work completely. Yet they tend to value the opportunity to work. Work provides financial security, a break from caring, a sense of identity and increased self-esteem. Increasingly, employers see the advantage of making career break schemes available to employees who need to care for a dependant or disabled relative rather than only to those who need to care for their children, particularly where the alternative would be to lose that person's skills for good. Career break schemes are dealt with in Chapter 9.

SAMPLE POLICY

Childcare Support Policy and Optional clauses

Policy
The Organisation adopts the following policy regarding childcare support for its employees.
1. *A childcare allowance is payable to any employee with dependent children for whom paid childcare provision is required during the periods the employee is at work.*
2. *The childcare allowance is payable for each child.*
3. *Where both parents work for the company, only one partner will be eligible to receive the allowance.*
4. *Where the employee works part-time, the allowance will be paid on a pro rata basis in line with the number of hours per week that the employee works.*
5. *The childcare allowance will be ___% of the actual cost of childcare up to a maximum of £___ a week.*
6. *The childcare allowance will be reviewed annually at the time of the salary review and the maximum weekly amount payable will be increased at least by the current inflation rate.*

7. *Applications for childcare allowance should be made in writing to _____.*

Optional clauses
- *No allowance will be paid where the employee's gross income exceeds £___ per annum.*
- *The childcare allowance will only be payable where evidence is supplied that the childcare is being provided by a registered childminder or nursery.*

KEY FACTS

- The availability of appropriate and good quality childcare is one of the most important forms of support that an employer can offer working parents.
- Workplace or employer sponsored nurseries, holiday play-schemes, childcare allowances or vouchers and after-school care can all play a part in simplifying working arrangements for employees who are parents.
- An unjustified refusal by an employer to agree to a woman's request to work part-time could lead to a claim for indirect sex discrimination.
- Employees are exempted from income tax on the benefit of nurseries provided by their employer either at the workplace or elsewhere on the employer's premises.
- Where nursery provision is not practicable, some employers may wish to provide childcare allowances or vouchers to their employees, although the former type of benefit is liable to income tax.
- A workplace nursery may be an expensive benefit to provide and its effectiveness depends upon the availability of a convenient location, one which is not too costly and which offers practicable travel to work arrangements for parents.
- The business case for introducing support for employees who look after frail, disabled or ill dependants of any age is every bit as valid as that for supporting employees with caring responsibilities for children.

CHAPTER 9

FLEXIBLE WORKING PATTERNS

INTRODUCTION

Historically, employers and employees have accepted that the standard or typical pattern of work was permanent full-time employment, most usually working from nine to five at the employer's premises. There was always a small proportion of the workforce employed on other arrangements but, particularly in the last 10 to 15 years, there has been a widespread expansion of what are appropriately referred to as non-standard or atypical working patterns. Together these are currently often referred to as flexible working patterns.

Flexible working patterns take the traditional notion of how work is organised and change it around. Flexibility often implies paying for the work that is done, and not for the worker's time. In other words, it should not really matter where and at what time of the day the work is done so long as it achieves the core business purpose as efficiently as possible. Once an employer begins to pay for the work, rather than the amount of time spent at work, they transfer to the employee the pressure of assessing how much time the work will take and where and how it can be done most efficiently.

This chapter aims to explore the most common recognised patterns of flexible working.

PART-TIME WORKING

In the UK an increasing number of people are choosing not to work full time. At the end of 2005, it was estimated that there were approximately 7.8 million people working part-time, of which approximately 77 per cent were women. Many part-time staff are working parents but others are people wishing to obtain a better balance between work and their personal lives. Part-time working is not new but has only relatively recently become subject to legislative controls, namely the **Part-time Workers (Prevention of Less Favourable Treatment) Regulations 2000**.

Definition of Part Time

There is no prescriptive definition of "full time" or "part time". A part-time worker is simply someone who works fewer hours than full-time employees within a particular organisation. For example, if the standard full-time hours within a particular organisation are 40 hours per week, then any employee who works fewer than 40 hours a week would be considered to be part time.

Advantages of Part-time Working

There are, arguably, many advantages for employers who facilitate part-time working patterns. Some of these are:

- the employer will have enhanced flexibility for covering peak times
- the employer will have the flexibility to extend their business opening hours (for example) to early mornings, evening and weekends
- it will be easier to arrange cover for holidays, sickness absence and other forms of leave because more people will be employed
- part-timers are less likely than full-timers to need time off work for medical appointments and the like
- the costs involved in paying for overtime can be reduced
- the employer will become an employer of choice able to attract many talented people who are only able to work on a part-time basis.

Statutory Rights of Part-time Employees

Part-time employees have the same statutory rights as full-time employees, ie they are entitled to benefit from all the legal provisions governing employment irrespective of how many hours they work per week or per month. Where a statutory benefit depends on the employee having a minimum period of qualifying service, no distinction is drawn between part-time and full-time service. For example, a part-time employee who works ten hours per week would gain the right to be protected against unfair dismissal after one year's continuous service in the same way as a full-time employee working (for example) 37 hours per week.

Part-time Workers (Prevention of Less Favourable Treatment) Regulations 2000

The **Part-time Workers (Prevention of Less Favourable Treatment) Regulations 2000** apply not only to employees but also to workers who work under a contract for services and who do not have employee status. This includes many atypical workers such as freelance people, casual workers, homeworkers and temporary staff. The Regulations do not, however, apply to the genuinely self-employed. There is no minimum period of qualifying service required for a worker to be entitled to the protection of the Regulations.

Under the Regulations, part-time workers have the right to be treated no less favourably than comparable full-time workers (on a pro-rata basis) with regard to both contractual terms and non-contractual policies, practices and benefits. This includes, for example, pay, holidays, benefits under an occupational sick pay scheme or occupational pension scheme, access to training and promotion and selection for redundancy. Treating a part-time worker less favourably than a comparable full-time worker will be unlawful unless the employer can justify the treatment on wholly objective grounds.

It can be seen from the Regulations that a wide range of benefits and treatments are covered. The non-discrimination principle would apply, for example, to promotion where it might be contrary to the Regulations to refuse to promote a particular employee because he or she works part time. In respect of training, the Regulations stipulate that part-timers must not be excluded from training just because they work part time.

Whilst part-time workers have the right to be paid at least the same basic hourly rate of pay as a comparable full-time worker, it should be noted that part-time workers are not entitled to enhanced overtime pay until they have worked the same number of hours as a comparable full-time worker. Differences in pay can, of course, be sustained if the reason for the difference has nothing to do with the fact that the worker in question works part-time, for example someone may be paid more because they have more experience, or because their performance has been shown to be better following an objective performance review.

Workers who consider that they have been treated less favourably because they work part time have to draw a comparison with an equivalent full-time worker. A comparable full-time worker is a worker who:

- works for the same employer on a full-time basis
- carries out the same or broadly similar work
- is employed under the same type of contract as the part-time worker
- works in the same establishment as the part-time worker or, if there is no comparable full-time worker at the same establishment as the part-time worker, at a different establishment within the same organisation.

Holidays and public holidays

All workers, including part-time workers, are entitled under the **Working Time Regulations 1998** to a minimum of four weeks' paid annual holiday, although of course this entitlement stands to be pro-rated for part-time workers. The four weeks statutory entitlement may be inclusive of public holidays as there is currently no statutory entitlement for any employees to be granted paid public holidays. The government has confirmed, however, that new legislation will require employers to grant workers eight paid public holidays over and above the four weeks of statutory annual leave. This is to be phased in; as from October 2007 workers will be entitled to four paid public holiday days per annum with the remainder being introduced at a later date. This does not mean that workers will have the right to time off on a particular public holiday, but rather that they will be entitled by law to additional days paid leave (over and above the statutory four weeks) at times to be agreed with the employer.

Where an employer offers its employees more than the statutory minimum holiday entitlement prescribed by statute, it must be sure to offer its part-time workers the same benefit on a pro-rata basis. For example, if the contract of a full-time employee who works five days a week stipulates that he or she will get 30 days' paid annual holiday, a part-time employee who works two days a week would be entitled to 12 days' paid holiday in a leave year. Similarly, if public holidays are granted in addition to annual leave, the employer must be careful that part-time employees are granted no fewer paid public holidays (on a pro-rata basis) than comparable full-time employees. For example, if an employer granted full-time employees 10 paid public holidays each year (over and above annual leave), then a part-time employee who worked half the week would be entitled to a minimum of five paid public holidays (or paid days in lieu) each year.

Switching from full-time to part-time work
The Regulations do not confer a right for an employee to demand part-time working, but rather give protection to those who do work part-time against unfavourable treatment. There is, however, a separate statutory right for employees who have parental responsibility for a child under the age of six to request "flexible working" (which includes part-time working) — see Chapter 10.

Under the Regulations, if it is agreed that a full-time employee will switch to part-time working in the same job, then the terms and conditions extended to that employee must not be less favourable on a pro-rata basis than those that applied as part of the previous full-time contract. Thus it is not permissible for an employer to make a move to part-time working contingent on an employee's agreeing (for example) to a lower hourly rate of pay. The same right applies to employees who, by agreement with the employer, return to work after a period of absence (for example, maternity leave) and at that time switch to part-time working, having previously worked full time. Assuming the employee remains in the same job and that it is only the hours of work that have changed, the other terms of the employee's contract must be no less favourable (again on a pro-rata basis) than the terms that applied when the individual worked full time. This right only applies, however, when the period of absence from work is no more than one year.

Enforcement of rights
Part-time workers who believe they have been denied their statutory rights under the Part-time Workers Regulations may request a written statement from their employer explaining the reasons for the alleged less favourable treatment. This must be provided to the employee within 21 days. Any statement provided (or a failure to provide a statement) will be admissible in evidence at an employment tribunal.

Part-time workers who believe that they have experienced unfavourable treatment on the grounds of their part-time status may also complain to an employment tribunal. There is no need for the part-timer to have any minimum period of qualifying service, or to resign first. Furthermore, if a part-time worker is dismissed for attempting to assert their rights under the Regulations, the dismissal will be automatically unfair.

Complaints to an employment tribunal must be presented within three months of the alleged less favourable treatment. If a claim is successful, the part-time worker will be awarded such compensation as the tribunal considers just and equitable in the circumstances, including compensation for any loss of benefit sustained as a direct consequence of his or her treatment.

SAMPLE POLICY STATEMENT

The Organisation recognises the important role that part-time employees can play in the workforce. It is prepared to employ part-time employees in jobs which can be done satisfactorily on a part-time basis, including those which can be done on a job-share basis. It will always consider requests from employees wishing to transfer from full-time to part-time work or vice versa, irrespective of length of service, age or family status.

JOB-SHARING

Job-sharing involves two (or more) employees each working part-time and carrying responsibility for the same job. The duties, hours, pay and benefits associated with the job are shared out between the job holders, pro-rated to the number of hours that each works. Job-sharing is now common in all sectors and all levels of employment. Job-sharing can bring many advantages as the employer will have the benefit of the skills, experience and work effort of two people rather than one.

Job-sharing Arrangements

The working patterns of two employees who are sharing a job can be agreed to suit both the employees and their employer. The options include:

- one job-sharer works mornings and the other afternoons
- the job-sharers work on separate days of the week
- the job-sharers each work alternate weeks
- the job-sharers agree between them when they will each work subject to the approval of their manager.

There is no rule that says that each of the job-sharers must work the same number of days or hours and it is open to all parties to agree whatever hours patterns suit the parties involved.

Contractual Issues

In job-sharing, each individual job-sharer has a separate contract of employment that should clearly define the following matters in addition to "normal" contractual terms:

- the working pattern, for example mornings only, two days a week, every alternate week, etc and the number of hours each job-sharer must work
- hand-over periods, ie where the two job-sharers are at work at the same time in order to facilitate smooth handovers and continuity
- whether there is any authority for the employer to vary the employees' hours of work according to the needs of the business
- whether the job-sharers are under a duty to cover for their partner's absences (for example holiday or sickness absence) in whole or in part
- pay, which must reflect the proportion of the full time position worked (this does not necessarily mean that each job-sharer must be paid the same amount, as pay may vary depending on (for example) experience
- holiday arrangements and rules about the job-sharers not being on holiday at the same time
- public holidays, ensuring that each job-sharer is granted the same pro-rata number of days as a comparable full-time worker, and that (assuming the hours of work are divided equally) one job-sharer does not benefit from more paid public holidays than the other
- access to training, taking care not to omit job-sharers from management and professional development
- what will happen if one job-sharer leaves as this needs to be addressed and understood by all job-sharers before the job-sharing arrangement is embarked upon.

When One Job-sharer Leaves

Assuming that there are two job-sharers and one leaves, the full time position should first be offered to the remaining job-sharer. If that job-sharer does not want to work full time, but would rather continue in the job-sharing arrangement, then another job-sharer should be sought by advertising the position (internally as well as externally) as part of a job-share. If this proves unsuccessful, redeployment of the remaining job-sharer to another part-time position should be considered and discussed. It will be important that this is allowed for in the contract. Only as a last resort should the remaining job-sharer be dismissed (in order to enable the employer to recruit a full-time employee into the position). This must be only after the employer has fully consulted with that employee and explored every possible avenue and alternative to dismissal.

Continuity of Employment for Job-sharers

For some job-sharers, there may be an issue of whether they gain continuity of service if, for example, the job-share arrangement is one week on and one week off. If this is the case the contract of employment should state that it governs every week, regardless of the number of hours worked, so that the employee's contract subsists throughout. This will avoid arguments at a later date.

COMPRESSED HOURS

Compressed hours means allowing employees to work fewer days each week, but longer hours on those days so that the same number of hours is worked over a shorter period. For example an employee may do a full time job over four days a week instead of five. Another pattern is the "nine-day fortnight" where employees have every second Friday (or second Monday) off.

Compressed hours can be of value to employees who wish to spend more time with their children at weekends, allowing them, for example, to take care of domestic chores on the Friday thus leaving them free on Saturday and Sunday to spend time with their children. This type of arrangement can also be beneficial to employees who work away from home, allowing them a longer weekend with their family.

TERM-TIME WORKING

Term-time working is an arrangement under which employees work a reduced number of weeks during the year and where the contract is set up specifically so that they are not required to work during the periods of the school holidays.

This is an annual contractual arrangement offered to employees who are the parents of school-age children where the parents need or want to be able to care for their children during school holidays. There has been a steady increase in this pattern of working over the last 10 to 15 years. It is becoming most common in occupations such as nursing and some parts of the retail sector.

A term-time working arrangement could accommodate either full-time or part-time working.

Continuity of Employment

Generally, the nature of term-time contracts is that the contract continues in force throughout the whole year, with the terms of the contract stipulating that the employee will not attend work during school holidays. By the very fact that the contract continues in place, continuity of employment is preserved.

In the event that it could be argued that the employee's contract of employment did not continue in force during the school holidays, the employee would still retain continuity of service by dint of provisions in s.212(3)(c) of the **Employment Rights Act 1996**. These provisions provide that if an employee is absent from work for a period of time as a result of an "arrangement" made with their employer, continuity of employment will be preserved despite the absence.

Contractual Issues

The contract of a term-time worker must be clear that the employer is not entitled to require the employee to carry out any work during the school holidays. This does not necessarily prevent the parties from agreeing between themselves at the time that the employee may perform some work during the school holidays, for example on a part-time basis.

It is important that the dates for determining school holidays are set out in the contract, particularly as different schools, in different areas, have varying dates of holidays. Agreeing the dates at the beginning of each school year is a sound idea.

Pay

There are two possible contractual arrangements for administering the pay of term-time workers.
1. Pay employees the normal weekly wage for the post during the weeks they work only, which means that periods of the school holidays when the employee does not work will in effect be unpaid.
2. Pay the employee an annual salary made up of twelve equal monthly payments, but with the annual rate being pro-rated down in proportion to the number of weeks the employee actually works.

If the latter arrangement is chosen, it will be important to have a clause in the contract that allows the employer to "claw back" any money overpaid in circumstances where the employee resigns towards the end of one of the school holiday periods.

Holidays

Employees on term-time contracts will, like all other workers, be entitled to a minimum of four weeks paid holiday per year. Most term-time contracts will state that annual leave must be taken during the school holidays, ie no further time off will be granted as annual leave. Thus, if the contract provides that the employee is paid only during the weeks when he or she is working (option 1 in the above sub-section), the employer will have to ensure that at least four of the weeks that fall within the school holidays are designated as holiday weeks and the employee's normal level of pay maintained during those weeks. If option 2 is chosen (ie paying the employee an annual salary made up of twelve equal monthly payments), the employer must add four weeks of annual leave to the number of weeks that the employee works in order to calculate their annual salary.

ANNUALISED HOURS

"Annualised hours" involves calculating working time on an annual basis and is a recent development towards greater flexibility in working patterns. It involves the employee working a minimum number of allocated hours during a year, but with flexibility in the actual hours worked on a week-to-week basis. The employee is usually paid an annual salary, divided into twelve equal monthly instalments, thus giving security of earnings irrespective of the number of hours worked in any particular month.

The key feature of an annualised hours arrangement is that the hours employees work may not be in a set pattern or amount for every week of the year. Shorter hours worked at one time of the year will be balanced out by longer hours worked at another time when the demand for work is higher. Each employee's contract should, however, specify the total number of hours that he or she is obliged to work over the year, allowing for holidays and public holidays, as well as making it clear that flexibility is required on a week-to-week basis as regards the number of hours worked.

Rules governing Annualised Hours

It is usual for the employer to specify certain "committed hours" that employees must work. These may represent a regular shift pattern, or may be variable. For example an employee may work 45 hours a week for short periods at peak times of the year and only 25 or less per week at other times. The hours that are rostered in this way are often known as "committed hours". Outside these committed hours, management can require the employee to work when the need arises, provided an agreed minimum period of notice is given. Such hours are often referred to as "reserve hours". An employer may wish to implement reserve hours during periods when there are seasonal peaks in the workload or when, for example, other employees are on annual leave or absent from work due to sickness.

An important issue to address is the minimum amount of notice to which an employee will be entitled when the employer wishes additional hours worked. The question of notice will of course relate merely to the reserve hours, as the committed hours will already be set.

A further related issue is the question of whether the employee is obliged to accept additional working hours (ie reserve hours) when asked to do them. An annualised hours scheme will usually provide that, if the minimum notice provisions are not complied with, there will be no obligation on the employee to accept the work, although some "give and take" should be exercised. It should also be made clear that no employee will be penalised on account of their inability to be available to work extra hours where inadequate notice has been given. Assuming, however, that the notice provisions are complied with, employees' contracts should make it clear that they are obliged to work reserve hours at the times requested.

Contracts of employment should also clarify what will happen if, at the end of the 12-month period, the number of hours worked by the employee does not coincide with the contractual annualised hours. Some schemes provide that an employee who has worked in excess of the annual hours will be entitled to take time off in lieu within a certain period, or alternatively to receive extra payment. Equally, if the employee has not reached the annual hours total, some schemes provide for a debit balance carry-over or a reduction in pay.

Overtime on Early Termination of the Contract

To prevent a dispute about what pay the employee will be due if he or she leaves part-way through the year, the contract should make it clear how hours and pay will be calculated in these circumstances. One method of dealing with this is to exclude payment of overtime, ie to provide that no extra pay will be due to an employee who leaves part-way through the year, irrespective of the number of hours worked so far that year. If this is not done, a clear method of calculating what extra payments (if any) will be due to the employee who is leaving, must be provided.

Similarly, the employer will have to decide how to calculate the pay due to an employee who leaves part-way through the year having not worked a sufficient number of hours in proportion to the number of months worked. The main issue will be whether the employer wishes to include a clause in employees' contracts permitting the employer to deduct a sum of money from an employee's final pay in these circumstances to account for the shortfall in hours worked. Again, a precise method of calculation would have to be devised.

Areas to be Addressed

The following areas will need to be considered and included in any annualised hours agreement:
- the definition of the "year" during which total annual hours will be counted
- whether any carry-over of hours to the next year (whether debit or credit) is allowed, and if so how many hours
- the number of hours employees will be required to work in a given period (the committed hours)
- any weekly or monthly minimum or maximum number of hours that employees may work
- how holidays will be dealt with
- whether employees are obliged to comply with a request to work reserve hours, or whether they may exercise a defined number of options to refuse
- the definition of any periods during which employees are required to be on call and thus available at short notice to come to work
- the minimum notice period that will be given to employees if they are called upon to work reserve hours

- any "protected periods", ie when employees will not be required to work under any circumstances
- how time spent working will be recorded
- a procedure to allow for calculation and reimbursement where employees leave at a time when they have been underpaid in relation to the number of hours they have worked so far that year
- contractual authority for the employer to reclaim any money paid to employees (including a precise method for calculation) who leave the company at a time when they have been overpaid in relation to the number of hours they have worked so far that year
- what will happen should an employee commence a period of leave, for example maternity leave or long term sick leave, at a time when he or she is in a credit situation in relation to the hours that he or she has worked.

HOMEWORK AND TELEWORK

There has been a considerable increase in recent years in the number of jobs that can be done wholly or partly at home. Homeworking is now so common that employees often say that working part of the time at home (away from the distractions of the workplace) is the only way to keep up with the volume of work.

The term "homeworking" is used to describe workers who are based at, or work from, home for one or more employer. Traditional homeworkers include piece-workers, sales people and the self-employed. "Teleworking" refers to those who spend part or all of their working time at home and who use computers and telecommunications equipment both to carry out their work and to maintain links with the workplace and their employer. There are, however, no precise legal definitions of the terms used although they can be given the above loose working descriptions.

The Benefits to the Employer of Employing Homeworkers

There are a number of potential benefits to employers who encourage homeworking, including:
- a reduction in the need for office space and an increase in the associated cost savings

- enhanced prospects for recruitment because the pool of prospective employees will include those who do not live close to the workplace and those who, for family reasons, cannot be away from home for lengthy periods
- time that would otherwise be spent commuting can be productive time instead (a feature that might be particularly attractive to many workers)
- reduced likelihood of absence from work for family reasons, as the employee will be at home anyway
- increased motivation and commitment to the organisation, assuming homeworking is managed effectively.

There are of course some disadvantages as well, as homeworking does not suit everyone and some people may find it difficult to manage and organise their own work, or be prone to distractions when working at home. There is also the issue of isolation. Many of the difficulties inherent in homeworking and teleworking can, however, be greatly reduced through proper planning, communication and the provision of regular management support.

Employment Status of Homeworkers and Teleworkers

Homeworkers and teleworkers may be employees of the organisation for whom they provide their services, or may technically be self-employed. Many traditional homeworkers may regard themselves as free to either accept or decline work from an employer and to accept work from other sources (which would indicate self-employment). In contrast, where a long relationship between a homeworker and an employer has developed, giving rise to expectations of regular continuing work, a relationship of employer and employee may exist. Another key relevant factor in determining employment status will be the degree of control and direction that the employer exercises over the day-to-day work of the homeworker, for example to what extent detailed and specific instructions are given as to how the work should be carried out.

Homeworkers may, of course work full-time or part-time and may work wholly from home, or partly at home and partly at the employer's premises. There is a great deal of potential for flexibility.

Contractual Issues

Certain provisions of an employer's standard contract of employment will be inappropriate for homeworkers and teleworkers. Equally, specific issues unique to those working at home will have to be addressed. For example, the contract should specify that the employee will be required to attend at the employer's workplace for such periods and for such purposes as the employer requires. This will, amongst other things, enable the employer to ensure that the employee does not lose touch through isolation. The contract should also include an express requirement for the worker to be available to attend all relevant training sessions and briefings, as required by the employer.

Pay
There are two possible methods of calculating rates of pay for employees who work at home.
- A fixed weekly or monthly wage/salary for a defined number of hours of work, with provision for overtime by agreement.
- A "fair piece rate" for each item produced or piece of work completed.
If the second option is chosen, the employer will need to comply with provisions in the **National Minimum Wage Act 1998** that require a "fair piece rate" to be worked out. This is done by carrying out a fair test of the number of hours that an average worker takes to produce a pre-determined number of items, then multiplying this figure by 120 per cent in order to establish the "deemed number" of hours. The wages paid to the worker must then be calculated by multiplying this deemed number of hours by the National Minimum Wage, and dividing the resultant number by the number of items previously identified. For example, if an average worker can produce five items in three hours, this three hours must be multiplied by 120 per cent, which results in a deemed figure of 3.6 hours. This deemed figure of 3.6 is multiplied by the National Minimum Wage, currently £5.35 (from October 2006) and the resultant figure (£19.26) divided by five. This would result in a minimum fair piece rate of £3.86.

Working hours, rest breaks and holidays
It needs to be borne in mind that homeworkers are entitled to the protection of the **Working Time Regulations 1998** and are therefore entitled to restrict their working hours to no more than 48 hours per week on average, take defined minimum rest breaks and be granted four weeks paid holiday leave each year.

Restrictions on working elsewhere

The employer will need to decide and include in the contract of someone who works wholly at home, a statement, as to whether or not he or she is permitted to perform paid work for any other employer. Any restriction should, of course, be reasonable and should not normally be imposed except in cases where the other job might adversely affect his or her work for the employer or create a conflict of interest.

Effective Management of Homeworkers

The effective management of homeworkers and teleworkers requires a different approach to that usually applied to the management of staff based at the workplace. It requires managers to "let go of the reins" and place a great deal of trust in the employee. It requires an acceptance of the fact that it is the homeworker, and not the manager, who will determine precisely when the employee will work, and how much they will do in, for example, a single day. Performance will usually stand to be managed by assessing output, and not the number of hours worked. Clear and fair targets will thus have to be agreed in respect of the work to be done if the arrangement is to be successful.

Health and Safety Issues

The contracts of all homeworkers should provide for the employer to be able — within reason — to enter the employee's home to check health and safety matters and engage in appropriate discussions with the employee on general work-related issues.

Employers have the same duties towards homeworkers and teleworkers to ensure their health and safety as they do in respect of employees based solely at the workplace. Whilst a full discussion of health and safety issues is outside the scope of this work, some of the main principles in respect of homeworkers can be summarised below. The employer's health and safety duties towards a homeworker will include:

- providing and maintaining safe equipment and safe systems of work
- ensuring the safe handling and storage of articles and substances
- conducting a suitable and sufficient analysis of the employee's workstation
- providing information and training on the safe use of display screen equipment

- providing the employee with the necessary information and training to use equipment safely
- ensuring as far as is reasonably practicable that third parties who may visit the employee's home for work-related purposes are not exposed to risks to their health and safety.

Moreover, risk assessments are required under regulation 3(1) of the **Management of Health and Safety at Work Regulations 1999** for every employee, regardless of where they are working. These require an assessment to be made not only of the risks to each employee's health and safety but also of the risks to others who are not employees, arising out of or in connection with the conduct by the employer of the undertaking. This could include potential risks to members of the employee's family or visitors to his or her home.

Confidentiality and Security

Homeworking also gives rise to a particular consideration regarding confidentiality and security. There may be a risk that confidential information may come to the attention of the employee's family, or even visitors to the home. In addition to the usual confidentiality provisions therefore, employees who work at home should be required to take certain defined precautionary measures to ensure that third parties do not have access to information and documents held by the employee, whether manually or on computer. Rules such as always keeping filing cabinets locked and passwords for the employee's computer will, for example, be essential. Ideally there should be a rule requiring the employee to agree that the computer they use for work-related purposes must not be used by any other member of the family at any time or for any purpose. A similar rule should apply to any other office equipment provided for the employee to work at home, for example a photocopier, printer, etc.

Another matter for the employer to address is the question of insurance — to ensure that both the employer's policies and the employee's home and contents insurance policies provide adequate cover for the fact that the employee works in their home.

FLEXIBLE WORKING HOURS AND FLEXITIME

Flexitime is a familiar concept. Essentially it is an arrangement whereby employees are required to work a pre-defined number of hours over a reference period (usually one month) but are offered limited flexibility over the times of day (or even days of the week) when these hours are worked. Although the actual mechanics of various schemes may differ, there are usually core periods, for example 10.00am to 12.00pm and 2.00pm to 4.00pm, during which employees must be at work, whilst each employee is given a degree of choice over when to work the remainder of their required contractual hours. This means that employees can choose, within defined limits, the times they start and finish work on different days of the week or in different weeks.

Such arrangements are particularly suitable for employees who have childcare or other domestic responsibilities.

The hours of work and the flexibility open to employees must of course be clearly specified as part of employees' contracts of employment, with a statement defining the maximum number of hours that may be worked each month and/or carried over from one reference period to the next. Employees will thus be allowed to build up surplus hours to a defined maximum number, and then take time off (known as "flexi-days").

Flexi-time schemes will need to define:
- the reference period, ie the period of time over which hours of work are counted (usually one month)
- core time, ie the hours during which employees are required to be at work
- flexible time which is the time during which employees can work flexibly, typically allowing start and finish times up to two hours before and after core time
- the degree of flexibility permitted at lunch times, ie minimum and maximum breaks allowed
- the maximum number of hours an employee may accrue in any given period, which are then taken as time off or perhaps even added to the employee's annual holiday entitlement
- overtime arrangements, ie whether overtime worked over and above standard contracted hours is paid, and if so at what rate
- how hours of work are to be recorded.

The Advantages of Flexitime

There are many benefits to employers and employees of operating flexitime which can:
- help to reduce problems of unsatisfactory timekeeping, as employees can make up for time if they arrive at work later than planned
- reduce travelling time because employees may be able to travel outside the rush-hour

- enable employees to arrange matters such as their personal business and medical appointments more easily
- relieve stress by removing the need to arrive at work at a precise time each day.

Flexible Working Hours

Even if an employer does not wish to operate a formal system of flexitime, that does not mean that they cannot or should not offer some flexibility to their staff over hours of work, and in particular start and finish times. Such flexibility will be a particular benefit to parents, allowing them to maintain a better balance between working time and their family responsibilities. Wherever possible, therefore, it is recommended that employers should give favourable consideration to the introduction of flexibility of working hours, whether as a formal scheme of flexitime, or in response to individual requests to work different hours. It may simply be a question of permitting a later or flexible start time in the morning for an employee who has to take children to school or wait for a childminder to arrive. Allowing this type of flexibility can take the pressure off an employee with family responsibilities by removing the worries about the risk of being late for work and perhaps even incurring disciplinary penalties. Often resistance to such flexibility in working hours is rooted in traditional working practices and attitudes that are no longer appropriate in relation to today's modern lifestyles.

Operating flexibly in terms of start and finish times can offer the employer considerable benefits in terms of employee morale and motivation. Conversely, refusing to grant simple requests to make marginal changes to employees' working hours may mean that the employer loses competent employees who choose to take their skills and expertise elsewhere to an employer who is prepared to operate more flexible working patterns.

In any event, employees who have parental responsibility for a child under six years old or caring responsibility for a dependent adult have the statutory right to request flexible working, which can include a request for different start/finish times (see Chapter 10).

SAMPLE POLICY

Flexible Working

Policy

The Organisation recognises that at various stages in employees' working lives, domestic and family commitments and responsibilities may potentially reduce or hinder their ability to fulfil work responsibilities. Where such conflicts arise and cannot be resolved, this could result in the Organisation losing employees. To prevent such loss of skilled, experienced workers, and to help reduce anxiety and stress among our workforce, this organisation not only acknowledges those potential conflicts but also offers practical help through its flexible working policy, based on the following key principles:

- *we will facilitate part time working (including job-sharing) in all jobs that can be done satisfactorily on a part-time basis*
- *we will always give fair and serious consideration to requests from employees to transfer from full-time to part-time work (or vice versa) irrespective of length of service, age or family status*
- *we will give full and fair consideration to requests for other working patterns including, for example, flexible working hours, term-time working, annualised hours and homeworking*
- *we will not impose any requirement for overtime hours on an employee if it would conflict with that employee's family needs*
- *where we agree to a new flexible working arrangement for an employee, this may be subject to a trial period of [ ] weeks/months prior to a final decision being made on whether or not the revised working pattern is workable.*

Employees interested in changing their current working hours or working pattern should discuss this initially with [ ].

KEY FACTS

- Part-time working has become increasingly popular in the UK, with the majority of part-timers (around 77 per cent) being women.
- Part-time employees have the same statutory rights as full-time employees, ie they are entitled to benefit from all the legal provisions governing employment irrespective of how many hours they work per week or per month.
- Part-time workers are entitled, under the **Part-time Workers (Prevention of Less Favourable Treatment) Regulations 2000**, not to be treated less favourably than comparable full-time workers (on a

pro-rata basis) with regard to both contractual terms and non-contractual policies, practices and benefits.

- Employers must ensure that part-time workers are granted equivalent annual holiday leave and paid public holidays as full-time staff on a pro-rata basis.
- Where it is agreed that a full-time employee will switch to part-time working in the same job, then the terms and conditions extended to that employee must not be less favourable on a pro-rata basis than those that applied as part of the previous full time contract.
- Job-sharing involves two (or more) employees each working on a part-time contract where, by agreement, the duties, hours, pay and benefits associated with the job are shared out between them.
- Term-time working is an arrangement under which employees work a reduced number of weeks during the year and where the contract is set up specifically so that they are not required to work during the school holidays.
- A term-time contract will continue in force throughout the whole year, notwithstanding the fact that the employee may not work for several weeks of the year.
- The employer may either pay a term-time employee a weekly wage during the weeks he or she works only, or pay an annual salary made up of twelve equal monthly payments, but with the annual rate being pro-rated down in proportion to the number of weeks the employee actually works.
- Annualised hours involves calculating working time on an annual basis and then scheduling employees to work a minimum number of "committed hours" whilst maintaining the right to require them to work additional "reserve hours" on a week-to-week basis.
- With an annualised hours arrangement, the hours employees work may not be in a set pattern or amount for every week of the year, and shorter hours worked at one time of the year will be balanced out by longer hours worked at another time when the demand for work is higher.
- There has been a considerable increase in recent years in the number of jobs that can be done wholly or partly at home.
- If the employer pays homeworkers on the basis of a "fair piece rate", the rate must be sufficient to satisfy the formula specified in the National Minimum Wage Act 1998.

- The effective management of homeworkers and teleworkers requires managers to "let go of the reins" and place a great deal of trust in the employee, and to measure performance by assessing output and not the number of hours worked.
- Employers have the same duties towards homeworkers to ensure their health and safety as they do in respect of employees based at the workplace.
- Flexitime is an arrangement whereby employees are required to work a pre-defined number of hours over a reference period (usually one month) but are offered limited flexibility over the times of day (or even days of the week) when these hours are worked.
- Even if employers do not wish to operate a formal system of flexitime, that does not mean that they cannot or should not offer some flexibility to their staff over hours of work, in particular with regard to start and finish times.
- Flexible working patterns can be of considerable benefit to employees who are parents. Offering flexibility will bring many advantages to the employer as well.

CHAPTER 10

RIGHT TO REQUEST FLEXIBLE WORKING

INTRODUCTION

Since April 2003, employees with parental responsibility for young or disabled children have had the right to formally request a change to their working arrangements in order to enable them to work more flexibly. Amendments to the law in April 2007 meant that employees who have caring responsibilities for adults also have the right to request flexible working. It is important to note, however, that eligible employees do not have an automatic right to work flexibly. Instead, those who qualify (see below) are entitled to *request* flexible working and the employer is then obliged to give that request serious consideration and follow through a defined procedure to review whether the request can be granted.

ELIGIBILITY TO REQUEST FLEXIBLE WORKING

In order to be eligible to request flexible working, the individual must:
- be an employee working under a contract of employment
- have at least 26 weeks' continuous service with his or her employer at the time the request is made

and must either:
- be the mother, father, adopter, guardian or foster parent of a child under the age of six (or age 18 if the child is disabled), or the spouse or partner of any of these (including same-sex partners) and
- live with the child, or

- be caring for an adult who is their spouse, partner, civil partner, parent, adult child (including adopted children), brother, sister, uncle, aunt, grandparent or someone else living at the same address (step-relatives and in-laws are included).

Requests for flexible working cannot be made more often than once a year.

TYPES OF REQUEST FOR FLEXIBLE WORKING

Employees who qualify are entitled to ask for a change to their terms and conditions of employment, including any or all of the following:
- the number of hours they work
- the times at which they are required to work
- their work location as between the workplace and their home.

Request could therefore be made for flexitime, job-sharing, part-time working, home-working, shift-working (or exemption from shift-working), exemption from overtime working, term-time working, etc.

Any agreed change to the employee's working arrangements will, unless expressly agreed otherwise, be a permanent change to their contractual terms. The employee will have no statutory right to revert to their original working pattern at any future date (although a further change may, of course, be agreed between the employer and employee at any time). The employer, similarly, has no statutory right to require the employee to revert to his or her previous pattern of working, for example once the child in question reaches six years of age.

Employee's Application

An employee who wishes to request flexible working must apply to the employer in writing (an e-mail or fax is acceptable). The application must:
- be dated
- specify that it is an application under the statutory right to request flexible working
- explain how the employee's relationship with the child or dependent adult meets the qualifying conditions
- set out details of the proposed change to the employee's pattern of working and when the employee would like this to come into effect
- explain what effects the proposal is likely to have on the employer and suggest how these effects might be dealt with

- state whether a previous application for flexible working has been made and, if so, when.

Technically, a request that does not meet the above criteria will not be valid (ie will not activate the statutory procedure), but it may nevertheless be in the employer's best interests to consider all requests, howsoever they are made.

PROCEDURE FOR CONSIDERING A REQUEST

An employer who receives a valid request for flexible working has a duty to give it serious consideration and follow a set procedure in doing so.

Within 28 days of receiving an application, the employer must hold a meeting with the employee to discuss it. However, if the employer agrees to the proposal in writing within 28 days, then there is no need to have the meeting. If the person who would ordinarily consider the application is absent on sick leave or annual leave, then the 28-day period may be extended.

The timing of the meeting must be convenient to both parties. The employee has the right to be accompanied by a fellow worker of his or her choice. This person may address the meeting and confer with the employee during the proceedings but is not allowed to answer questions on the employee's behalf. If the employee's chosen fellow worker cannot be present at the time proposed for the meeting, then the employer must rearrange the meeting for another date, which must be within seven days of the original date and at a time that is agreeable to everyone.

At the meeting itself, the employee's proposed new working pattern should be discussed fully with a view to seeing how it might be made to work. All relevant issues should be explored. If there are potential problems with the employee's request, the employer should be prepared to consider possible alternative arrangements that might suit both the employee's personal needs and the needs of the business. Both parties should be willing, if necessary, to consider a compromise.

Within 14 days of the meeting, the employer must write to the employee with a decision. If the employee's proposal is accepted, then the employer must set out the new working pattern and when it will take effect. If the employer refuses the request, then the letter must give the reason (see below) and an explanation of why that reason applies in the employee's case.

REASONS FOR REFUSING A REQUEST

An employer is only permitted to refuse a request for flexible working if one of the reasons listed below applies in the particular case. It is not open to employers to invent their own reasons. The valid reasons for refusal are:

- burden of additional costs
- detrimental effect on ability to meet customer demand
- detrimental impact on quality
- detrimental impact on performance
- inability to reorganise work among existing staff
- inability to recruit additional staff
- insufficient work during the hours the employee proposes to work
- planned structural changes.

The letter to the employee must also explain the appeal procedure.

Appeals

If an employee's request for flexible working is refused, the employee must be granted the right to appeal against the decision. To do so, the employee must write to the employer within 14 days of receiving the decision setting out the grounds of appeal. Within 14 days of that date, the employer must hold another meeting with the employee to discuss the appeal. Once again, the time and place of the meeting must be convenient to both parties and the employee has the right to be accompanied by a fellow worker of his or her choice. The appeal must, of course, be dealt with by a different manager (ideally someone more senior) to the person who made the decision to refuse the employee's request.

The employer must subsequently give the employee a written decision within 14 days of the appeal hearing. If the appeal is upheld, then the letter should set out the change agreed to and the date when this will come into effect. If the appeal is dismissed, then the letter must set out the grounds for refusal and explain why those grounds apply to the employee's case.

Time Limits

Any of the time limits that are laid down for different parts of the procedure may be extended by agreement between employer and employee.

If both parties agree to extend any of the time limits, then the employer must ensure that the agreement is recorded in writing, specifying the date on which the extension is to end.

ENFORCEMENT

An employee whose request for flexible working is refused may complain to an employment tribunal, but only in limited circumstances. These are where the employer:

- failed to follow the statutory procedure for dealing with the employee's request for flexible working (for example, if the employer failed to arrange a meeting within the set timescale)
- rejected the employee's application on grounds other than the permitted reasons
- based its decision on incorrect facts.

Employees are not entitled to apply to a tribunal simply because they disagree with the employer's decision. Provided the employee's request has been given proper consideration and the procedure has been followed, a tribunal is not allowed to question the validity of the employer's decision or substitute its own opinion for that of the employer.

If a tribunal finds in favour of an employee, it may order the employer to reconsider the application and/or make an award of compensation. The maximum amount of compensation is eight weeks' pay (subject to the statutory limit on a week's pay, which is currently £310).

An employer and employee with a dispute over a request for flexible working may agree to refer the matter to the Advisory, Conciliation and Arbitration Service (ACAS) for arbitration.

DETRIMENT OR DISMISSAL

If an employee is dismissed or disadvantaged at work because he or she has made, or intends to make, a request for flexible working, he or she may make a complaint to an employment tribunal. Dismissal on such grounds will be automatically unfair. No qualifying service is needed to bring a claim for unfair dismissal in these circumstances.

SAMPLE POLICY

Flexible Working Policy and Procedure (Parents and Carers)

Policy

The Organisation's Flexible Working Policy outlines the organisation's commitment to consider flexible working arrangements for the parents of young, adopted or disabled children, and to employees who have caring responsibilities for adult relatives.

No employee will be treated less favourably, suffer detriment, or be dismissed because they request flexible working or move to a different working pattern under this policy.

Flexible working is about considering the way work is organised to see whether it is possible to agree to different arrangements, whilst taking into account the organisational and technical needs of the company.

Employees should be aware that if they request and are granted a change to their working pattern, this will be a permanent variation to their terms and conditions of employment. Thus if their circumstances change in relation to the need for flexible working, there will be no statutory or contractual right for them to return to their previous terms and conditions. This does not, of course, prevent the employee from requesting another change, but simply means that there will be no automatic right for them to have that request granted.

Procedure

To be eligible to request flexible working, a person must:
- be an employee of the organisation
- have worked for the organisation continuously for 26 weeks at the date of the application for flexible working
- live with and have parental responsibility for a child under [ ] years of age, or be married to or the partner of a person with such responsibility, or
- have caring responsibility (or joint responsibility) for an adult relative or other person who lives in the same household.

When making a request for flexible working, the employee should provide the following information in writing:
- the flexible working pattern that they would like
- the date on which they would like the change to come into effect
- their relationship with the child or adult relative
- the effect, if any, they think the proposed change would have on the Organisation (for example on their colleagues' work) and how, in their opinion, any such effect might be dealt with.

The application should be given or sent to [ ], and should be signed and dated.

KEY FACTS

- Employees with parental responsibility for one or more children under the age of six (or age 18 where the child is disabled) have the right to request flexible working.
- Employees who have caring responsibilities for an adult who is their spouse, partner, civil partner, parent, adult child, brother, sister, uncle, aunt, grandparent or for someone else living at the same address also have the right to request flexible working.
- Employees do not have an automatic right to work flexibly, but rather the right to request flexible working and have their request considered seriously by means of a defined procedure.
- To be eligible to request flexible working, the employee must have at least 26 weeks' continuous service with their employer.
- Employees who qualify are entitled to ask for a change to the number of hours they work, the times at which they are required to work and/or to do some or all of their work from home.
- An employer is only permitted to refuse a request for flexible working if the reason for refusal is one of a defined list of reasons.
- An employer who receives a valid request for flexible working must hold a meeting with the employee to discuss the request and how it might be made to work.
- If an employee's request for flexible working is refused, the employee must be granted the right to appeal against the decision within 14 days.
- If an employee is dismissed or disadvantaged at work because he or she has made, or intends to make, a request for flexible working, he or she may make a complaint to an employment tribunal.

Index

A

absenteeism
reducing.. 11
additional maternity leave *see*
maternity leave
additional paternity leave 47–8
adoption
parental leave and............... 65, 66, 73
paternity leave and...... 43, 44, 49, 50
adoption leave................................ 1, 51
additional adoption leave 51
eligibility...................................... 62–3
rights and duties during............. 56
rights on return....................... 59, 63
timing and duration 54
contracts of
employment and.............. 54, 56, 63
detriment...................................... 59, 63
dismissal...................................... 59, 63
disrupted placements...................... 56
duration 51, 54, 62
duties during.................................... 56
eligibility........................... 51, 52, 62–3
foster parents and........................... 52
"keeping in touch days" 57
legal requirements 51–2
length................................. 51, 54, 62
notification requirements........... 52–3
change of start date...................... 53
employer's response 54
ordinary adoption leave 51
eligibility.. 62–3
rights and duties during 56, 63
rights on return...................... 58, 63
timing and duration 54
overseas adoptions............. 52, 53, 54
qualifying conditions........... 52, 62–3
resignation... 58
right to return 57–9, 63
early return................................. 57–8
sickness at end of leave 58
rights during................................. 56–7
sample policies........................... 59–62
sickness at end 58
step-parents and.............................. 52
timing 54, 63
adoption pay *see* statutory adoption
pay
age discrimination............................. 89
ageing population 2
Alabaster v Woolwich plc & another
[2004]... 20
allowances
childcare.................................. 101, 105
annual leave *see* holidays
annualised hours 5, 6, 116, 127
committed hours.................... 117, 127
contracts of employment............. 117
notice...................................... 117, 118
overtime on early termination.... 118
reserve hours................. 117, 118, 127
rules.. 117
shift working.................................... 117
see also flexible working
antenatal care
amount of... 15
evidence of appointment.............. 15
part-time staff................................. 15

refusal of 15
remedies for refusal 15–16
rights 39
sample policy 35
shift workers 15
time off 14–16
see also maternity

B

benefits
career breaks, during 90, 91
childcare allowances
    and vouchers 101, 105
maternity leave,
    during 22, 29, 40
part-time working 126–7
workplace nurseries 99
breastfeeding facilities 34

C

career breaks 85–6
advantages 86
age discrimination 89
application procedures 90–1, 96
benefits during 90, 91
continuity of employment 87–8
contracts
    of employment 87–9, 94, 96
contractual issues 90–1, 94, 96
disadvantages 86
eligibility 90
Employment Rights Act
    1996 .... 87, 88, 94
grounds for 90, 96
keeping in touch 91, 96
law and 87
length 96
notice of return 91
part-time workers 89, 96
pensions 91, 94
policy 90, 91
    sample policy 93–5
redundancy 87

refusal 91
returning to work 92–3, 96
    notice period 91
sabbaticals 86, 87
sex discrimination 89
staying in touch 91, 96
terms and conditions of
    employment 91
training during 92
working during 92
    for other employers 92
    unpaid work 92
    voluntary work 92
case studies
childcare 103
maternity 33–5
**Chartered Institute of Personnel and
Development (CIPD)**
work-life balance 7–9
child tax credit 101
childbirth
establishing date of 29–30
expected week of 18, 29
meaning 18
see also maternity
childcare 97
allowances 100–1, 105
best practice 101–2
case studies 103
employers initiatives 99–101
nursery provision 99, 105
part-time working and 97, 98
partnership provision 103
provision 97–8
sample policy 104–5
sex discrimination 98, 105
tax treatment 99–101, 105
vouchers 100–1, 105
workplace nurseries 99, 105
Children Act 1989
parental responsibility 66
collective agreements
parental leave 67, 69, 72–3, 74

committed hours *see* annualised hours

compassionate leave 81–2, 95
  circumstances
    for grant............................ 81–2, 83–5
  duration...................................... 83, 95
  Employment Rights Act
    1996...................................... 81, 82
  personal/family difficulties 83–4
  policy............................ 81, 82–3, 95
    sample policy................................ 85
  sick child, caring for 84–5, 95
  see also dependants
compressed hours...................... 5, 114
confidentiality
  homework and telework 123
continuity of employment
  career breaks................................ 87–8
  Employment Rights Act
    1996 .... 87, 88, 94, 115
  job-sharing.................................... 114
  term-time working........................ 115
contract for services
  non-discrimination principle 109
contracts of employment
  adoption leave 54, 56, 63
  annualised hours.................. 117, 118
  career breaks 87–9, 94, 96
  homework and telework 121–2
  job-sharing..................................... 113
  maternity leave................... 21, 29, 40
  parental leave 69
  paternity leave 46, 50
contractual issues
  career breaks 90–1, 94, 96
  homework and telework 121–2
  job-sharing..................................... 113
  term-time working 115, 127
contractual maternity pay............... 22
contractual rights
  maternity 27, 29, 32–3
  parental leave 71
Creating a Work-Life Balance 5
customer retention..................... 10

customer satisfaction 10

D

demographic changes 2
dependants, time off
  to care for 1, 2, 75, 104, 105
  circumstances for grant 76–7
  definition of "dependant"............. 76
  detriment 75, 78, 79
  dismissal 75, 78, 79
  duration...................................... 76, 79
  Employment Rights Act 1996....... 75
  enforcement 71–2
  entitlement 75–7
  legal requirements 75
  length.. 76, 79
  notice requirements........................ 77
  sample policy................................. 78–9
  see also compassionate leave
detriment
  adoption leave............................ 59, 63
  dependants, time off
    to care for........................... 75, 78, 79
  flexible working,
    request for 133, 135
  maternity 25
  parental leave............................ 72, 74
  paternity leave 44, 50
disabled children
  parental leave...................... 66, 73, 74
discrimination *see* sex discrimination
dismissal
  adoption leave........................... 59, 63
  dependants, time off
    to care for........................... 75, 78, 79
  flexible working,
    request for 133, 135
  job-sharing................................. 113–14
  maternity, connected with....... 26, 41
  parental leave............................ 72, 74
  paternity leave 44, 50
  temporary maternity
    cover.................................... 25–6, 34

dismissal and disciplinary
procedure (DDP) 26

E

elderly relatives 2, 11
employees *see* staff
employment contracts *see* contracts
of employment
Employment Equality (Age)
Regulations 2006 89
Employment Rights Act 1996 16
career breaks 87, 88, 94
compassionate leave 81, 82
continuity of
employment 87, 88, 94, 96, 115
time off to care for dependants.... 75
employment terms *see* terms and
conditions of employment
employment tribunals
antenatal care 15–16
parental leave 72
part-time workers 111–12
expected week of childbirth
(EWC) 17, 18, 29, 36, 40
meaning 18

F

family-friendly policies 1
best practice 2–7
business case 7–11
legal requirements 1
productivity and performance 10
recruitment and 9
recruitment tool 9
reducing absenteeism, sickness and
stress 11
reputation as good employer 11
retention of staff 9–10
staff morale, commitment and
loyalty 10–11
work-life balance and 2, 3, 4–7
fathers
role 2

transfer of maternity leave to 27
see also paternity leave; statutory
paternity pay
Finance Act 1990 99
Fixed-term Employees (Prevention
of Less Favourable Treatment)
Regulations 2002 26
flexible working 1, 4, 9–11,
107, 111, 125, 128
flexitime *see* flexitime
request for 1, 25, 129
appeal against refusal 132, 135
consideration procedure 131
detriment 133, 135
dismissal 133, 135
eligibility 129–30, 135
employee's application 130–1
enforcement 133
parental responsibility 111, 125,
129, 134, 135
reasons for refusing 132–3, 135
time limits 132–3
types 130–1
sample policy 126, 134–5
flexitime 5, 123–5, 128
advantages 124–5
hours of work 124
overtime 124
foster parents
adoption leave and 52

G

*Gillespie and others v Northern
Ireland Health and Social Services
Board and others* (1996) 32

H

health and safety
homework
and telework 122–3, 128
pregnant
employees 16–17, 28, 39–40
risk assessments 16, 31, 123

holidays
  accrual during additional maternity
    leave.. 22
  homework and telework 121
  job-sharing.. 113
  part-time workers.................... 110–11
  public holidays 110–11, 113
  term-time working......................... 116
homework
  and telework 5, 8, 119, 127–8
  benefits to employers 119–20
  confidentiality................................. 123
  contracts of employment......... 121–2
  contractual issues........................ 121–2
  disadvantages.................................. 120
  employment status 120
  "fair piece rate" 121, 127
  health and safety
    issues 122–3, 128
  holidays 121
  hours of work................................. 121
  insurance 123
  management............................ 122, 128
  meaning of "homeworking" 119
  meaning of "teleworking".......... 119
  overtime.. 121
  pay.. 121, 127
  restrictions on
    working elsewhere...................... 122
  risk assessments 123
  security 123
  training............................ 121, 122, 123
HSBC Bank plc
  nursery provision........................... 103

I

individual agreements
  parental leave 67, 70, 72–3, 74
insurance
  homework and telework 123

J

job-sharing................ 4, 5, 10, 112, 127
  arrangements 112

continuity of employment........... 114
contracts of employment............. 114
contractual issues.......................... 113
dismissal 113–14
holidays.. 113
hours of work......................... 112, 113
leaving a job-share................. 113–14
pay 113
public holidays 113
training.. 113
variation.. 113

K

"keeping in touch days"
  maternity leave............................. 22–3
  paternity leave................................... 57

M

Management of Health and Safety
  at Work (Amendment) Regulations
  1994 .... 31, 35
Management of Health and Safety
  at Work Regulations 1992 35
Management of Health and Safety
  at Work Regulations 1999.... 16, 123
maternity 13
  antenatal care *see* antenatal care
  breastfeeding facilities.................... 34
  case studies 33–5
  childbirth
    establishing date of................ 29–30
    expected week
      of (EWC) 17, 18, 29, 40
    meaning 18
  contracts of employment......... 29, 40
  contractual rights 27, 29, 32–3
  detriment.. 25
  dismissal...................................... 26, 41
  expected week of childbirth
    (EWC).......................... 17, 18, 29, 40
  health and safety
    considerations 16–17, 28, 39–40
  leave *see* maternity leave

141

legal requirements 14
night work 16, 31, 39
notification
   requirements 17–18, 28
pay *see* maternity pay
policy 28–34
   sample policies 35–9
redundancy and 23
risk assessments 16, 31
sex discrimination
   claims 22, 23, 25, 29, 33
suspension
   from work 16–17, 31, 40
maternity leave 14
additional maternity leave 17
   case study 33
   contractual benefits
     during 22, 29, 40
   contractual rights 27
   duration 17
   entitlement 40
   holiday accrual during 22
   intentions regarding return 30
   length 17
   obligations during 22
   pay rise during 25
   redundancy and 23
   rights during 22, 29
   rights on return 25, 30–1, 41
automatic trigger 19, 22, 40
benefits during 22, 29, 40
case study 33
change of start date 18
childbirth, meaning 18
compulsory maternity
   leave period 17
continuous service 27, 41
contracts of employment 29, 40
contractual benefits
   during 22, 29, 40
contractual rights 27, 32–3
dismissal connected with 26, 41
dismissal of temporary
   replacements 26, 34

duration 17
entitlement 40
expected week of childbirth
   (EWC) 17, 18, 36, 40
factory workers 17
future developments 27–8
intentions regarding return 30
"keeping in touch days" 22–3
length 17
notification
   requirements 17–18, 28
   change of start date 18
   employer's response 18
   right to return 23–4, 40
ordinary maternity leave 17
contractual benefits
   during 22, 29, 40
   duration 17
   entitlement 40
   intentions regarding return 30
   length 17
   redundancy and 23
   rights during 22, 29
   rights on return 24, 30–1, 40–1
part-time work,
   return to 25, 31, 32, 33, 41
pay increase during 20, 25, 32
proposed increase 27
redundancy and 23
resignation during 24
return date 18
right to return 23–5
   notification 23–4, 40
   part-time basis 25, 31, 32, 33, 41
   same job, same rights 30–1, 40–1
   sickness at end of leave 24
rights during 22, 29
rights on return 24–5, 30–1, 40–1
sickness at end 24
start date 18
   automatic trigger 19, 40
   notification of change 18
temporary replacements ... 26, 34, 41
timing 18–19, 40

transfer to father 27
Maternity and Parental Leave
  Regulations 1999 65
maternity pay
  contractual 22
  statutory *see* statutory maternity
  pay
maternity policy 28–34
  sample policies 35–9

N

National Minimum Wage Act
  1998 .... 121, 127
night work
  pregnant employees 16, 31, 39
nurseries 99, 105

O

ordinary maternity leave *see*
  maternity leave
outworking *see* homework and
  telework
overtime
  flexitime 124
  homework and telework 121
  part-time workers 109
  termination of annualised hours
    arrangement 118

P

parental leave 1, 65
  a week's leave, meaning 67
  adopted children 65, 66, 73, 74
  best practice 72–3
  change of employer 67
  collective
    agreements 67, 69, 72–3, 74
  contracts of employment 69
  contractual rights 71
  detriment 72, 74
  disabled children 66, 73, 74
  dismissal 72, 74

duration 65, 66–7, 73
eligibility 65, 66, 73
employment tribunals 72
enforcement 72
fallback scheme 67, 70–1, 73, 74
individual
  agreements 67, 70, 72–3, 74
legal requirements 65
length 65, 66–7, 73
maximum period of leave
  per year 70
minimum period of leave 70
notice 67–8, 70–1, 74
obligations during 68
postponement 71
qualification 65, 66, 73
record keeping 71–2
right to return 68, 74
rights during 68
schemes 69–71
timing 66–7
workforce
  agreements 67, 69, 72–3, 74
Part-time Workers (Prevention of
  Less Favourable Treatment)
  Regulations 2000 .... 89, 98, 108,
                          109–12, 126–7
part-time working 108, 126–7
  advantages 108
  antenatal care 15
  benefits 126–7
  career breaks 89, 96
  childcare responsibilities and 98
  employment tribunals 111–12
  enforcement of rights 111
  holidays 110–11
  meaning of "part-time" 108
  overtime pay 109
  pay 109
  pensions 109
  promotion 109
  public holidays 110–11
  redundancy selection 109
  return after absence 111

return from maternity leave
   to 25, 31, 32, 33, 41
sample policy statement 112
sex discrimination 98
statement of reasons for less
   favourable treatment 111
statutory rights 108–9
switching from
   full-time work 111, 127
terms and conditions of
   employment 109, 126–7
training 98, 109
unfair dismissal 109
paternity leave 1, 43
   additional paternity leave 47–8
   adoption and 43, 44, 50
   contracts of employment 46, 50
   detriment 44, 50
   dismissal 44, 50
   duration 45–6, 47, 50
   eligibility 44, 50
   legal requirements 43–4
   length 45–6, 47, 50
   notification requirements 45
   qualifying conditions 44, 50
   right to return 46
   sample policy 48–9
   terms and conditions during 46
   timing 45–6, 50
paternity pay *see* statutory paternity
   pay
pay
   homework and telework 121, 127
   increase during
     maternity leave 20, 25, 32
   job-sharing 113
   part-time workers 109
   term-time working 115–16, 127
   see also maternity pay; statutory
     adoption pay; statutory maternity
     pay; statutory paternity pay
pension rights
   career breaks and 91, 94
   part-time workers 109

performance
   work-life balance and 10
pregnancy *see* maternity
productivity
   work-life balance and 10
public holidays
   job-sharing 113
   part-time working 110–11

R

record keeping
   parental leave 71–2
records
   statutory maternity pay 21
recruitment
   family-friendly policies and 9
   retention and 9–10
redundancy
   career breaks 87
   maternity and 23
   part-time workers 109
reserve hours *see* annualised hours
retention of staff 9–10
risk assessments
   homework and telework 123
   maternity 16, 31

S

sabbaticals 86, 87
   see also career breaks
security
   homework and telework 123
self-employment 109, 119, 120
sex discrimination
   career breaks 89
   childcare and 98, 105
   indirect 25, 98, 105
   maternity and 22, 23, 25, 29, 33
Sex Discrimination Act
   1975 .... 25, 33, 89, 98
shift working
   annualised hours 117
   antenatal care 15

flexible working 130

sickness
  at end of adoption leave 58
  at end of maternity leave 24
  reducing 11

small employers
  statutory adoption pay 55
  statutory maternity pay 21
  statutory paternity pay 47

staff
  morale, commitment
    and loyalty 10–11
  retention 9–10

statutory adoption pay
  (SAP) 47, 51, 52, 54–5, 63
  recovery 55
  small employers 55

Statutory Maternity Pay (General)
Amendment Regulations 1996 32

statutory maternity pay
  (SMP) 19–21, 22, 47, 54
  calculation 20
  entitlement 19, 20, 22, 40
  exclusions 29
  expected week of childbirth
    (EWC) 29
  medical evidence 21
  pay rises and 20, 32
  payment 19–20, 29
  rates 20
  records 21
  recovery 21, 32
  small employers 21

statutory paternity pay
  (SPP) 43, 46–7, 50, 54
  future developments 47–8
  recovery 47
  small employers 47

statutory sick pay (SSP)
  sickness
    at end of adoption leave 58
  sickness
    at end of maternity leave 24

step-parents
  adoption leave and 52

stress
  compassionate leave 82
  flexitime and 125
  reducing 11, 125

suspension from work
  maternity grounds 16–17, 31, 40

Suspension from Work (on
Maternity Grounds)
Order 1994 31

T

telework *see* homework and telework

temporary
  maternity cover 25–6, 41
  dismissal 26, 34

term-time working 4, 114–15, 127
  continuity of employment 115
  contractual issues 115, 127
  holidays 116
  pay 115–16, 127

terms and conditions of
employment
  career breaks 91
  part-time workers 109, 127
  paternity leave 46

training
  career breaks 92
  costs 9
  homework
    and telework 121, 122, 123
  job-sharing 113
  part-time workers 98, 109

U

unfair dismissal
  adoption leave 59, 63
  dependants,
    time off to care for 75, 78, 79
  flexible working,
    request for 133, 135
  maternity 26, 41
  parental leave 72, 74

part-time workers.................... 111–12
paternity leave 44, 50
temporary maternity cover..... 26, 34

V

voluntary work................................... 92
vouchers
for childcare...................... 100–1, 105

W

"Who Cares Wins" 3
Work and Families, Choice and
Flexibilities 4

work-life balance 2, 3, 4–7
CIPD Factsheet.............................. 7–9
Creating a Work-Life Balance 5
performance and............................. 10
productivity and 10
workforce agreements
parental leave 67, 69, 72–3, 74
working tax credit 101
Working Time
Regulations 1998 .... 110, 121
workplace nurseries................. 99, 105

146